Think About This

A collection of 50 original
Primary School Assembly Stories

Written by David Webb
Illustrated by Robert Mirfin

Introduction

David Webb has been a Head Teacher in three different primary schools and has gained a wealth of experience in presenting primary assemblies. David is a well known writer of children's fiction and this brand new collection of stories is guaranteed to appeal to children of primary age.

Each story comes complete with an identified theme, a closing prayer, follow up activities and suggestions for subsequent assemblies. The stories are lively, thought provoking and often humorous.

"Think About This Story" provides ideal support for collective worship, also for use in delivering moral and social education in the classroom.

Think About This Story

First Published in February 2001.

Printed and Published by

PUBLISHING

© David Webb

ISBN10: 1 900818 51 5
ISBN 13: 978 1 900818 51 3

Educational Printing Services Limited
Albion Mill, Water Street, Great Harwood, Blackburn BB6 7QR
Telephone: (01254) 882080   Fax: (01254) 882010
E-mail: enquiries@eprint.co.uk   Website: www.eprint.co.uk

CONTENTS

contents continued

FROM SMALL ACORNS

Theme: Growing up / the right conditions for growth.

Introduction: Hold an acorn up in assembly and ask the children if they know what it is. When you have confirmed that it is an acorn and that it is a seed, ask what it would grow into if it were planted. Where would be a good place to plant the acorn? How would it need to be cared for as it grows? Explain that the acorn will only grow into a strong and healthy oak tree if it is given the right conditions.

Sam and David were twins and they were just six years old. It was a beautiful autumn morning - a clear, bright blue sky and warm October sunshine. Their grandfather decided that it would be a good morning for a walk and they set off towards the Town Park. Grandad knew that there were lots of grey squirrels in the park and it was just the sort of day that they would be busy gathering their store for winter. They took a footpath along the side of some houses and before long the park gates were in sight.

Once inside the park, the two boys ran ahead. There were leaves everywhere, golden brown, deep red, vivid orange. Sam and David ran through them so that they crackled and crunched beneath their feet. They kicked them up into the air and laughed as they showered down onto their heads. Grandad walked behind, smiling in satisfaction as he watched the two boys enjoying themselves.

After a while, the two boys raced towards a large oak tree that stood alone in the centre of a playing field. Around the base and spreading out for some distance, were hundreds of acorns. The two boys gathered them up in their hands. They were small and hard and very shiny. Neither Sam nor David knew what they were.
'What are these funny nuts?' asked David. He was the more inquisitive of the twins. He was always asking questions.

'They're called acorns,' explained Grandad, picking one from the floor and holding it in the palm of his hand. 'They're the fruit of the oak tree. They grow along with the leaves during the spring and summer and then they fall in the autumn, just as the leaves do, so that the oak tree can take its winter rest.'

The two boys looked up at the great oak tree as a few more golden brown leaves drifted slowly to the ground.

'If you plant an acorn and if you look after it and care for it when it grows, one day it will form a huge, strong tree, just like the one before us. It's like a lot of things in life, given the right conditions it will turn out fine.'

'Can we plant an acorn?' asked David. 'Can we see if it grows into a tree?'

'Of course you can,' said Grandad, 'but it's up to you to look after them.'

That afternoon, the two boys carefully planted their acorns into pots and stood them in a sheltered spot at the bottom of their garden. Grandad explained that they would need to be left all winter, that nature would take its course and the acorns would start to shoot when the warmer weather of spring arrived.

Sure enough, the following spring, two small

green shoots poked through the dark soil. David was delighted when he saw the new growth. Sam was pleased at first but he soon lost interest. David checked his plant pot every few days. He moved it to another part of the garden so that it could benefit from the warm sunshine. When the weather was dry, he watered his plant. He showed his Grandad how well it was growing. Before long it sprouted leaves and it really began to look like a small tree.

'A young tree is called a sapling,' explained Grandad. 'Your sapling looks very healthy. It should grow into a fine oak tree. Maybe next year we can plant it in the garden or, better still, find a place in the park where it will have more space to grow.'

And so they did. The following spring David and his Grandad took the young sapling to the park keeper who was only too pleased to plant it in a position where it would thrive.

David was pleased and proud and he visited the park regularly to check on its progress.

But what about Sam's acorn? Well, the plant pot was still there in the garden, exactly where he had left it, but there was no sign of life. The young shoot had withered and died from lack of care and attention and Sam had long forgotten all about the small shiny acorn.

Funnily enough, as the years passed and the two boys grew older, David got on far better in life than his twin brother. He worked hard, had lots of friends and generally enjoyed life. Sam couldn't really be bothered. He was content to drift along without really giving much effort to anything. David still returned to the park, usually each spring, and every time he looked at the young oak tree, growing taller and stronger each year, he remembered his Grandad's words: 'Given the right conditions it will turn out fine.'

Prayer: Dear Lord, give us the right conditions for growth. Help us to work hard and do our best in everything we do. May we respect all living things and appreciate the wonderful world that you have made. Help us to grow up to be kind, caring and considerate people. Amen.

Follow up: Choose some reliable children to plant acorns. You may even want to plant some in pots at the end of assembly. Decide where to leave the pots over winter, preferably within the school grounds. Decide on a date in spring when the children can check the pots for signs of growth. Mark the date in your diary as a reminder.

Class teachers may wish to look at other autumn seeds or this can form part of a follow up assembly. Is there an entrance area to the school where a collection of autumn seeds could be displayed along with relevant observational drawings and written work?

HENRY THE HEDGEHOG'S AUTUMN FRIGHT

Theme: Danger/Environmental Awareness

Introduction: Use this story in late autumn to link with other assemblies about dangers the children might encounter. Ask the children why they have to be particularly careful when travelling to and from school when the mornings and evenings are dark. Talk about danger from the traffic and remind the children about 'stranger danger'. Stress how important it is, if children are not collected by an adult, to go straight home after school. Explain to the children that it is not only humans who face added danger at this time of year. Some animals encounter troubles of their own.

It was late autumn and Henry the hedgehog was feeling tired. On the whole, it had been a good summer. The weather had been rather wet as usual but at least it had been warm and wet. However, the last few weeks had turned really cold, especially at night-time. At first there was a biting, easterly wind that whipped up the leaves and blew dust into Henry's hedgehog eyes. Once the wind dropped the frost arrived, covering the ground in glistening white crystals, making Henry shiver and scamper for shelter in his bed of leaves. He woke up one morning to a covering of snow. It was fairly thin and it didn't last long but it made Henry realise, it was time to prepare for hibernation.

Henry knew that he had to choose his bed carefully. There were so many dangers in the world for unsuspecting hedgehogs. Why, it was only the previous autumn that he had almost been flattened by a huge truck whilst visiting his cousin Horace!

He began his search for a safe place to sleep. Henry remembered that he had visited a garden where there was a most comfortable pile of leaves. The house owner had obviously collected them together and left them in a convenient heap for Henry. How thoughtful. It took him a while to find the garden, especially as he stopped to eat a few juicy slugs on the way, but once he was there he was convinced that it was the perfect nest for hibernation. He burrowed deep into the pile, twisting round until he was comfortable, and then he settled down and closed his eyes in readiness for sleep. He was just dozing off when he was disturbed by a most annoying collection of noises. There were voices, human voices, and a strange brushing sound, as if more leaves were being heaped onto the pile.

'Can we light the bonfire now?' enquired a young voice. It was the daughter of the house, eager to help her father do some tidying up in the garden.

'Yes, let's get it started,' confirmed father, and he stooped down and struck a match.

Henry, of course, couldn't understand a word they said, but he soon noticed a pungent, smoky smell and his soft bed was getting a little too warm for comfort. He rushed out of the leaves as fast as his little legs would carry him, his heart thumping with fright.

'Oh, look!' cried the little girl, pointing after the scurrying hedgehog. 'What a good job he got away before the fire took hold.'

'Good job, indeed!' thought Henry. 'I was nearly a roasted hedgehog!'

Henry was feeling depressed. He walked slowly from garden to garden muttering to himself.

'I can't go near the road because of the traffic; I can't sleep underneath a hedge because of those silly electric trimmers the humans use and now I can't even settle beneath a pile of leaves! Where is a poor hedgehog supposed to hibernate?'

Henry stood still and stared around in despair. And then he saw it. An old garden shed that was raised on a wooden platform, leaving a gap beneath that was just wide enough for a hedgehog to crawl into.

'Perfect!' thought Henry, cheering up immediately. 'Warm and dry and surely fire-free!' He poked his nose beneath the shed and was delighted to find a layer of leaves, blown there by the autumn winds.

'Just the job!' confirmed Henry, and he crawled under the shed into the warmth and the semi-darkness.

Henry had made a nest of leaves within minutes. He put his head down, closed his eyes and drifted off into wonderful autumn sleep, dreaming of bright sunshine and warm spring days.

PLANTING BULBS

Theme: Things that grow

Introduction: This story is best used in October when some of the children may be planting bulbs in class. Have some different types of bulbs ready to show the children. Begin by asking what they are. Having established that they are bulbs, ask the children if they can name any flowers that grow from bulbs. Hopefully, they will name some of the examples you have brought in and you will be able to match the bulb to the name. Some pictures of the flowers would be useful. Ask when most bulbs flower and talk about the cycle of Nature - most bulbs are planted in autumn, they begin to grow over winter, they flower in spring, they rest in summer.

'Now then, who can tell me what a bulb is?'

Mrs. Matthews was standing in front of her Year 2 class. She was holding a cardboard box and the children were eager to know what it contained. Several hands shot into the air and Mrs. Matthews waited for a moment before deciding who to ask.

'Yes, Wesley,' she said, smiling at a dark haired boy who was waving his hand about enthusiastically. 'Are you going to tell me what a bulb is?'

'Yes, Mrs. Matthews. It's made of glass and you stick it in a light socket and it makes the room bright when you flick the switch.'

'Very good,' said Mrs. Matthews, with a faint smile. 'And you are quite right, Wesley - but I wasn't thinking of a light bulb, I was thinking of a different type of bulb. Would anyone else like to give me an answer?'

Once again, several hands shot up. Mrs. Matthews chose more carefully this time.

'Yes, Melanie,' she said, confident of a sensible answer.

'It's a kind of plant, Mrs. Matthews. We've got some daffodils in our garden and they're bulbs.'

'Excellent,' said Mrs. Matthews, smiling back at Melanie. 'A bulb is a kind of plant. There are many different types of bulb, aren't there, and I've got some different bulbs in this box. Let's have a look at some, should we?'

Mrs. Matthews reached into the box and pulled out a couple of tiny bulbs, almost white in colour. She held them up for the children to see, gripping them carefully between her thumb and forefinger.

'Now then,' she said, using her favourite words. 'What do you think these bulbs are? I'll give you a clue. They flower earlier than any of the other bulbs in my box. They produce little white flowers, sometimes as early as February.'

'I know what they are,' said Wesley, not waiting to be asked. 'They're snowdrops. My mum says she knows spring is on the way when she sees the first snowdrops.'

'Good boy, Wesley. They are snowdrops, but don't shout out, next time. Wait to be asked. See if you know this next bulb.'

Again, Mrs. Matthews put her hand in the box and pulled out a bulb, still quite small but a little larger than the snowdrops. She held it up for the children to see.

'These bulbs also flower early,' explained the teacher. 'They come in lovely, bright colours. The most common are purple, yellow or white but you sometimes see stripey ones.'

'I know those, too,' said Wesley, and the other children tutted and stared at him for shouting out. 'They're crocuses, Mrs. Matthews. I like the stripey ones best.'

'OK,' said Mrs. Matthews. 'Now, it's someone else's turn this time, Wesley.'

In went the hand and Mrs. Matthews pulled out a daffodil bulb.

'You see more of these in spring than any other bulb,' said Mrs. Matthews. 'Lovely bright yellow flowers that grow in the wild as well as in parks and gardens.'

'Daffodils,' whispered Wesley, and Lisa Davies dug him in the ribs.

And so the lesson went on. Mrs. Matthews showed the children a tulip bulb and a large, purple hyacinth and then she explained how the bulbs had to be planted if they were to grow successfully.

'I've got some bulb fibre and we're going to plant them in pots,' said Mrs. Matthews. 'When we've planted them, we'll water them and put them into a dark cupboard. That will encourage them to grow. They'll stay in the cupboard until Christmas and then, once they start to shoot, we'll bring them out and put them on top of the cupboard so that they get plenty of light. You'll be able to see the shoots turn green. The stems will grow and the buds will begin to form. As they begin to flower, we'll move them into the school entrance area so that everyone can enjoy them.'

'What will we do with them when they're dead?' asked Wesley.

'The bulbs won't die,' explained Mrs. Matthews. 'The flowers will fade but the bulbs won't die. We'll take them outside and plant them in the school grounds. They'll rest through the summer. Next autumn they'll start to shoot all over again and, if they're not disturbed or damaged, they'll flower again the following spring!'

'That's brilliant!' said Wesley. 'Much better than a light bulb! Can we start planting them, Mrs. Matthews?'

'Come on, then,' said the teacher, smiling. 'I think we'd better get on with it.'

Prayer: Help us, Lord, to appreciate the wonders of Nature. Help us to care for all living things - the plants, the animals, and the people around us. As we live our daily lives, may we never do anything to harm the wonderful world that you have given us. Amen.

Follow up: Choose some children to plant and care for the bulbs that you brought in to assembly. Try to follow the timescale outlined in the story, bringing the bulbs back into assembly every so often to show their progress. If all goes well, display them in a prominent place as they come into flower. Plant them in the school grounds ready for the next season.

OFF FOR THE WINTER

Theme: Autumn/Migration

Introduction: This is a good assembly to give towards the end of September. Begin by discussing the changes that occur as we move from summer into autumn. Ask the children to identify the various signs of autumn. Someone is bound to mention hibernation. Ask the younger children what the word means and identify animals that hibernate. If the word migration has not been given, ask the children what some birds do in autumn. See if the children can name any birds that migrate. You may wish to finish the introduction by stating that you would quite like to fly south for the winter!

It was a clear, crisp Sunday afternoon towards the end of September. The weather had been lovely for the past few days, bright and sunny but clearly getting colder, with the first hint of frost showing in the early mornings. Rachel and her brother Carl were out walking with their mum. There was a lodge near to where they lived, a long stretch of water that was once used to supply the nearby cotton mills but was now mostly used by the local fishing club. If the weather was dry, it was possible to walk right round the edge of the lodge. It took about forty-five minutes.

'Autumn can be a lovely season,' said mum, as they ambled along the dirt track. 'I love autumn when the weather's clear and bright.'

'Why wasn't it like this in summer?' grumbled Carl. 'It rained most of the time we were on holiday.'

'Just look at the trees,' continued mum, ignoring Carl's comment. 'Look at the lovely colours. Reds, golds, yellows . . . '

'We've been looking at autumn leaves at school,' interrupted Rachel. 'Mrs. Williams said we could collect different types of leaves and take them into school.'

'Well, you see how many different types of leaves you can find as we go round,' said

mum, 'then when we get home we'll see if we can identify them.'

'I want to see the swans,' said Carl. 'Last time we walked around the lodge there were two swans and three baby swans. I think their nest was just around the next bend.'

'They're called cygnets,' said Rachel. 'Baby swans are called cygnets.'

'They might have left by now,' said mum. 'It is autumn, don't forget.'

'What do you mean left?' asked Carl. 'Where would they have gone?'

'They might have migrated,' explained mum. 'Lots of birds migrate for the winter. They fly south to find warmer weather. They stay there all winter and then, when spring arrives and our weather begins to warm up again, they come back to this country. The swans might fly thousands of miles but they'll still find their way back to this lodge next year. They're very clever. I don't know how they do it.'

'What's that noise?' said Rachel. She had stopped in her tracks and she was listening intently.

'I think I know what you can hear,' said mum. 'Let's walk on a bit and you'll soon see where the noise is coming from.'

A few minutes later, when Rachel, Carl and mum had walked past where the swans had nested, a strange sight met their eyes. Ahead of them, in the middle of a field, was a large, metal electricity pylon and it was absolutely covered with birds. They looked restless and agitated. They were chattering and screeching, flying backwards and forwards relentlessly. There were hundreds of them.

'What are they doing?' asked Carl. 'I've never seen so many birds gathered in one place!'

'They're swallows,' explained mum. 'You can tell by the shape of their tails. They're getting ready to migrate. They all gather together like that before they fly off for the winter.'

'It's brilliant!' said Rachel. 'I didn't realise that birds were so clever. When will they go?'

'They'll go when they're ready,' said mum. 'They could go today, very soon. They often pick a fine, clear day - better conditions for travelling, you see.'

'I want to see them take off,' said Carl. 'It would be like a big, black cloud.'

'Some birds fly in formation,' explained mum. 'Geese, for example. You can see them make a pattern in the sky. One bird leads the way and the others all seem to know their places in the pattern.'

The swallows seemed to be getting noisier than ever. The din was deafening.

'Why don't we migrate for the winter?' asked Rachel. 'I thought we were supposed to be cleverer than birds.'

'We humans have too many responsibilities,' said mum. 'Imagine going into school and telling your teacher you were flying south for six months. Bye, Mrs. Williams! See you next spring!'

'I should think she'd like that,' said Carl. 'Get rid of her for six months!'

'Come on,' said mum. 'We could stand here all day. It might be a few days before the swallows take off. They're just preparing themselves, getting ready for the long flight. Let's keep going shall we? Let's collect some leaves and look out for other signs of autumn.'

Prayer: Thank you, Lord, for the lovely season of autumn. Help us to appreciate the wonder of nature. Thank you for the falling leaves with their wonderful colours. Thank you for the autumn fruits and berries and for the crops that make up the harvest. Thank you for the birds and the animals that never cease to amaze us. Thank you for the lovely season of autumn. Amen.

Follow up: Migration is a fascinating topic. Ask the children to find out about other birds that migrate. Where do they go? Apart from the fact that the weather is cold, why do some birds choose to migrate? (Longer daylight hours, food supplies, breeding conditions etc.).

Keep a watch for migrating birds gathering or passing over the school.

Discuss what could be done to help the birds that stay in Britain during the winter. How could birds be encouraged to visit the school grounds?

DARK DAYS

Theme: Coping with and staying safe in the dark days of winter

Introduction: The beginning of December is a good time to give this assembly. Ask the children: 'Who finds it difficult to get up these dark mornings?' Many hands are sure to rise - probably including staff! It is always easier to get up on a summer morning when the sun is shining. Explain that when the mornings are so dark it still feels like night and it seems almost unnatural to get up. In December, there are some days when it does not get properly light at all. You wake up in the dark and by the time school has finished, you go home in the dark. The good news is that it doesn't last too long and, even during the dark days, there are things that we can all look forward to.

It was the third time Lewis's mum had called him. He yawned and stretched under his warm, comfortable covers before shoving his head out of the top and shouting down in a sleepy voice, 'I'm coming, mum!'

It was the beginning of December and the mornings were pitch black. Lewis hated them. It was difficult enough to get up in summer but it was unnatural to get up when the mornings were so dark. He waited a few more minutes before stumbling out of bed and reaching for his socks. He wobbled to the bathroom, his eyes only half open, and when he swilled his face the water was an unwelcome shock to him.

'Will you get a move on!' shouted mum. 'Your breakfast is on the table!'

At eight thirty, there was a knock on the door. Lewis always walked to school with his friends, Danny, Sarah and Matt. Mr. Briggs, the Headteacher at Lewis's school, had warned the children not to walk to or from school on their own during the dark winter days - it was too dangerous.

As they set off for Park Lane Primary School, it seemed darker than ever. It was a damp, drizzly December morning and the thick clouds meant that there was no sign of the rising sun. It was about a fifteen minute walk to school and only when they were in the playground did the day finally begin to break. The whistle sounded and the children left the dismal playground for the bright lights of the school.

That morning, in school assembly, Mr. Briggs talked all about Advent. He explained to the children that Advent was the time leading up to Christmas and that, although the short days meant darkness, it was a time to look forward to a new light in the world. He asked the children to look around the hall at all the bright and colourful decorations and at the lovely green fir tree with its twinkling lights. One class had made a large Advent calendar, which had been put up as part of the hall display. Mr. Briggs chose a little girl called Melanie to open the door for the day. Melanie was really excited and, when she pulled open the door to reveal a great brown spotted Christmas pudding, she couldn't stop giggling.

'I love Christmas pudding,' said Mr. Briggs, rubbing his tummy. 'You see - that's something I'll be looking forward to eating on Christmas Day!'

Mr. Briggs promised that on the last day of term, when school finished for the Christmas holiday, he would choose children to open all the remaining doors. He also explained that after Christmas, when the children came back to school, the days would gradually start to get lighter.

The children could not go out to play that morning break. The rain had become heavier and the playground looked darker than ever.

It was the same story at lunchtime. By home time, any remaining daylight had once again disappeared. Lewis pulled on his coat and set off for home with his friends. He knew he would find it just as hard to get up for school on Monday morning - but it would soon be Christmas. Two whole weeks off school! Two whole weeks when he could lie in! He grunted to himself in satisfaction. Perhaps the dark days of winter were not that bad after all.

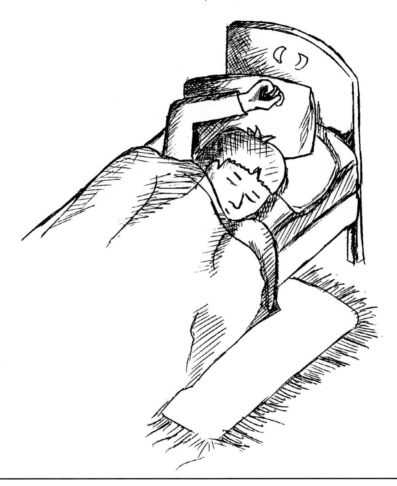

Prayer: Lord, help us through the dark days of winter. Keep us safe from all danger. May we remember the guiding light that you sent into our world and may we fulfil our lives by following your teaching. Amen.

Follow up: Remind the children of the dangers they could face during the dark days of winter. Remind them to be aware of traffic, particularly when approaching and departing from school. Reinforce what they should do if ever approached by a 'stranger'. Remind them also to go straight home after school has finished.

The children could make their own Advent calendars using pictures from old Christmas cards. Alternatively, make a large Advent calendar for the school hall. The doors could be opened each assembly, as in the story.

DON'T LEAVE THE LIGHT ON

Theme: Energy conservation/caring for the environment

Introduction: It would be useful to give this assembly on a dark morning or afternoon. Have all the lights switched off in the assembly area so that the children are sitting in semi-darkness. Ask if anyone notices something strange about assembly. What would be a good thing to do before assembly continues? When somebody suggests that more light would help, have someone switch on the lights. Explain that there are times when it is absolutely necessary to have the lights on but there are times when leaving them turned on is wasteful. See if anyone can tell you why it is wasteful to leave lights on in an empty room. Yes, the electricity bill is higher but it is also using up a valuable resource.

'You've done it again!' stormed Jamie's dad.

He had just returned home from work to find every light in the house switched on, the television on and a C.D. blaring out from the player. Jamie was nowhere in sight. He appeared suddenly, on the stairs, with a drink in his hand.

'Hi, dad. Had a good day?'

'Yes thanks,' replied dad, curtly. 'How many times do I have to tell you - when you leave a room turn the light off! And what's the point of having the television on when you're not in the room watching it?'

'I've only been upstairs for half an hour,' explained Jamie. 'I'd just have to switch everything back on again, wouldn't I?'

'The point is,' said dad, slowly, 'that you are wasting electricity. You wait until you have to pay the bills. You're just as bad with the gas fire. If you're the last out of the room you never turn it off!'

It was true. Jamie was awful. He just did not see it as a problem and he used to drive his parents mad. One day he left the tap running and flooded the bathroom. The first anyone new about it was when water dripped through the kitchen ceiling onto dad's head. Even Jamie realised what a blunder that was - the bathroom took days to dry out.

It was only when Jamie began a new topic at school that he began to realise there was a point to dad's protests. The children entered class one dark afternoon to find all the lights switched off. Jamie immediately went to turn them on but Mrs. Briggs, the class teacher, told him to leave them alone and sit down. Jamie looked puzzled.

'Before we begin work this afternoon,' began the teacher, 'I want you to tell me why it is important to switch lights off when they are not needed?'

Jamie knew the answer, really. His dad had explained it to him so many times.

'That's right,' continued Mrs. Briggs, after a few children had responded. 'To save money on electricity bills but, more importantly, to conserve energy. I bet if we take a walk around school we will find lots of areas with lights switched on where they are not really needed. Jamie - go and have a look in the school hall.'

Jamie left the classroom and took the short walk to the school hall. He was back within a minute.

'The lights were on, Mrs. Briggs, and there was no one in the hall.'

'All those lights left on to light an empty hall! What did you do about it, Jamie?'

'I switched them off,' replied Jamie, proudly.

'Well done,' said Mrs. Briggs. 'Now I bet it is the same in your homes - lights and televisions left on in empty rooms. If only one of you remembers to switch things off it won't make a great deal of difference. However, if each and every one of you in this class starts to turn off unnecessary lights that would make a difference. And if everyone in this school and then everyone in other schools did the same we would really conserve energy.'

The children nodded in agreement. Jamie could really see her point.

'Using up the world's resources is causing untold damage to our planet,' continued Mrs. Briggs, 'so we are going to do our bit to help. We are going to become energy savers. We'll begin with classroom light monitors and we'll choose someone to check the hall each morning and afternoon. Let's see if we can do our bit to save the planet!'

Jamie was chosen to be the hall monitor. That evening, he began at home. He glanced into the kitchen and, seeing the lights on, he switched them off.

'Hey!' yelled dad. 'Do you mind! I'm eating my dinner!'

'Sorry, dad,' said Jamie, flicking the switch back on. 'I was just saving the planet!'

Jamie's dad coughed, spluttered and nearly choked with shock.

Prayer: Help us, Lord, to look after this wonderful world that you have given us. We know that human beings are using up and destroying natural resources. May each and every one of us do all we can to protect the environment and preserve our planet for future generations. Amen.

Follow up: The assembly can be used as a starting point for energy conservation in school. Each class can appoint 'light monitors'. Make it a child's job to turn the lights off in the school hall after assembly.

Identify other sources of energy waste in school. For example, are taps left running? Are paper towels wasted? Are doors left open allowing heat to escape?

The children could design posters with an energy conservation theme. The finished posters could then be displayed in key areas throughout the school.

Discuss how homes and schools coped before there was any gas or electricity? Think of all the things people would not be able to do. It is hard to imagine life without these modern sources of energy.

WHAT HAVE YOU LEARNED TODAY?

Theme: Knowledge

Introduction: Begin by telling the pupils about something you have learned recently. It could be how to do something new on the computer, some knowledge about a person or event - even a new route to school you have recently discovered. Explain that you learn something new every day - you never stop learning. Ask the children how they learn. This should promote some interesting discussion. They learn from teachers, from parents and friends, from books, computers and from the T.V. They also learn from experience - and they sometimes learn the hard way. Explain that sometimes knowledge is just acquired but that more often you have to work hard in order to learn.

Jordan walked in through the door and threw his bag down onto the kitchen floor as usual.

'Hello,' said Dad, putting his newspaper down. 'Have you had a good day at school today?'

'Not bad, thanks,' replied Jordan. He flung his jacket over the back of a chair and headed for the fridge. 'I'm starving. Really thirsty, too.'

'What have you learned today?' asked Dad. 'Anything interesting?'

'Nothing,' mumbled Jordan, removing the milk container and reaching for a glass.

Dad looked a little puzzled. Jordan never drank milk. He usually poured himself a large glass of fizzy cola.

'You mean you've spent a whole day at school and you haven't learned one single thing? I don't know what schools are coming to these days. Don't they teach you anything?'

Jordan shrugged his shoulders and poured out a large glass of milk. He gulped it down in about six seconds and then wiped his mouth on the back of his hand.

'Lovely,' he said, rinsing his glass in the sink. 'Milk's very good for you, you know. It's full of vitamins and calcium. Very good for building strong bones and white teeth. I found that out in Science today. Our teacher, Mrs. Fraser, told us all about foods that are good for you and foods that are bad for you. I'm going to drink milk from now on instead of cola.'

'Well, I'm pleased to hear it,' said Dad, smiling.' Your mum will be in from work soon. We'll see about eating a healthy tea when she arrives home.'

'No hurry,' said Jordan. 'There's a T.V. programme I want to watch. We're reading a book in literacy and the same story is being shown on T.V. in six parts. Mrs. Fraser said to make sure we don't miss it. We're going to talk about it in school tomorrow.'

'Fine,' said Dad. 'I'm pleased you're so keen.'

Secretly, he was hoping to have watched the racing on Channel 4 but he carried on reading his paper instead.

'It's all about some children who were evacuated during the Second World War,' continued Jordan. 'We've just started a project about the Second World War today. It's really interesting. Were you evacuated during the war, dad?'

'I'm not that old!' said Dad, offended. 'But I think your Grandad was evacuated. You'll have to talk to him about it next time you see him.'

'I think I'll write him a letter,' said Jordan, thoughtfully. 'We've been learning how to set out a letter properly in class today. Yes, I'll sit down this evening and write him a letter.'

Jordan picked a banana out of the fruit bowl and settled down on the sofa to watch his T.V. programme. He paused the sound briefly to explain to his father just how good bananas were for you. They boosted the potassium levels, according to Mrs. Fraser. Jordan made a few notes on a pad as he watched the programme. He kept nodding with satisfaction and at one point he muttered, 'Ah, yes! We learned that today?'

Jordan's mum returned home from work just as the programme finished.

'Hello,' she said, cheerily, putting her bag down by the door. 'Have you both had a good day?'

'Yes thanks,' said Dad.

'Not bad, thanks,' said Jordan. He picked up his banana skin and aimed it towards the bin.

'And what have you learned today, Jordan?'

'Nothing!' said Jordan, and the brown banana skin flew through the air and landed on the carpet.

Prayer: Thank you, Lord, for the wonderful gift of knowledge. Thank you for those who teach us and for those who produce the books, the programmes and the equipment that helps us to learn. May we also learn to follow your example and grow up to be kind, caring and considerate people. Amen.

Follow up: Discuss what it means 'to learn the hard way.' Explain that people do make mistakes but that it is important to learn from those mistakes.

Discuss how methods of learning have changed over the years. Ask the children how they imagine people learned before radio, T.V. or computers were invented. New technology, such as the Internet, means that many pupils have greater opportunity to learn at home. Ask the children if they think new technology means that people will use books less? What might schools be like in the future? Will there be any need for teachers?

BEST FRIENDS

Theme: Friendship

Introduction: Choose two children to bring out to the front of the assembly who always play together. Ask the rest of the children why they think you have selected the two children. Explain that it is not because of the way they look or the way they work. It is because they are best friends who always get on well together. Ask the children what qualities they look for in a friend - someone you can trust, honesty, reliability, a sense of humour etc. You would not choose a friend who you know would let you down.

Laura and Hannah were best friends. They had been best friends since the very first day they started at school. Mrs. Wade, the Reception Class teacher, had sat them next to each other and they had been difficult to part ever since. The two girls did everything together. Laura would call for Hannah first thing in the morning and they would make the short journey to school together, talking about what was on television the previous evening, or what was going to happen during the day. They still sat next to each other in class and, whenever their teacher said that people could work together, the two girls were the first to co-operate. They even shared the same hobbies. They went to swimming club on the same night, they read the same books and they liked the same music. Mrs. Groom, their Year 5 teacher, called them 'the twins', even though they looked nothing like each other. The two girls were really happy in each other's company. Happy, that is, until a new girl arrived at school.

It was a Tuesday morning and the Year 5 children had just started their numeracy lesson when Mrs. Pritchard, the Headteacher, walked into the classroom with two adults and a nervous looking girl.

'I want to introduce you to Lucy,' she announced. 'Lucy has just moved into the area. She is starting school today and she is going to be in your class. Now, I want you to help her settle in. Show her just how friendly we are at St. Phillip's School. Is that clear?'

'Yes, Mrs. Pritchard!' chorused the children, and the new girl glanced up, shyly.

Mrs. Groom found Lucy a place to sit next to Laura and she asked Laura to show her where to hang her coat in the cloakroom. Hannah wished she could have gone with the new girl but she didn't say anything.

Just as morning play was approaching, Mrs. Groom chose Hannah to do a job, tidying up some books on the class library shelf. It meant that she could not go out at the same time as the other children and she looked on in envy as Laura and Lucy left the classroom together. By the time Hannah had finished her job, playtime was nearly over. She went out into the yard and looked around for Laura but she was nowhere to be seen. It was only when the bell sounded that her friend came from around the corner of the building, laughing and chatting with Lucy.

'Had a good time?' asked Hannah, as Laura and Lucy walked straight past her.

'Oh, yes thanks,' replied Laura. 'Lucy's really nice. I just know we're going to get on together.'

Hannah scowled as the two new friends stood next to each other in the line. She had never felt like this before. She felt let down and left out. Laura was her friend and Lucy had no right to take her away.

The day got no better for Hannah. She followed Laura and Lucy through the canteen at lunchtime but when she came to sit down, there was no place left on the table. She ended up sitting next to a group of younger boys who spent the whole time talking about football. Hannah looked on in envy as Laura and Lucy chatted away to each other, apparently becoming more and more friendly.

By home time, Hannah felt really miserable. Laura had hardly spoken to her all day. To make matters worse, Mrs. Groom had let Laura and Lucy go and get their coats from the cloakroom early, just until Lucy got used to the routine. She decided that she hated Lucy and that there was no way she was going to talk to her. Hannah was jealous and she really did not like the feeling. She was

just about to walk home alone when she felt someone grab hold of her arm. She turned round to see Laura staring at her, a concerned expression on her face.

'What are you doing?' asked Laura. 'Surely you were going to wait for me? We always walk home together.'

'Thought you might have walked home with your fancy new friend,' snapped Hannah. 'Where's she disappeared to all of a sudden?'

'Don't be stupid,' said Laura. 'She's not my fancy new friend, as you put it. She's very nice, but you're my best friend. She could never replace you.'

Hannah softened a little. She looked down at the ground and said, 'It's just that you've spent the whole day with her. You've hardly spoken to me.'

'Just think how you would feel if you went to a new school and you didn't know one single person. Surely you'd want someone to look after you until you settled in?'

'Well, I suppose so,' admitted Hannah. 'If you put it like that.'

'You wouldn't like me as a friend if I just didn't care how people felt, would you?' continued Laura. 'I wouldn't be the sort of person you'd want to know.'

'I suppose not,' said Hannah, and she forced a thin smile. 'I've been a bit stupid, haven't I?'

'Not really,' said Laura, and she put her arm around her best friend's shoulder.

'I think I know how you were feeling today. I tell you what, why don't we both call for Lucy on the way to school tomorrow morning? Why don't we both show that we care about her?'

'Good idea,' agreed Hannah. 'After all, we always do everything together, don't we Laura?'

Prayer: Help us, Lord, to be kind and considerate people who always consider the needs of others. Help us to value friendship and to treat our friends with respect. Help us to choose our friends carefully and for the right reasons. May we always have the courage to say no when others try to lead us astray. Help us to realise that you are always there for us and will never let us down. Amen.

Follow up: The children could write a poem entitled My Best Friend. The poem could be about all the qualities that they would look for when choosing a best friend.

The older children could discuss the concept of peer pressure. Has anyone ever been tempted to do something they know to be wrong just because their friends put pressure on them? Discuss how important it is to choose friends carefully.

A TRIP TO MARKET

Theme: Taking advice

Introduction: Have you noticed how some people think they always know best, even if others are better informed? As you grow up you are still finding your way in life and, if you want to know something or you need some advice, there is usually someone with more experience who you can turn to. You should never be too proud to seek or to accept advice.

Farmer Grimes was a stubborn man who only ever took notice of his own opinion. As a result, he had few friends and his neighbours did not really bother with him.

One cold, wet Monday morning in late November, Farmer Grimes looked in his larder and saw - empty shelves.

'I've got to get to market,' he thought to himself, as he looked out of the farmhouse window at the steadily falling rain. 'It can't be avoided - I've got to get to market.'

So the farmer put on his great coat and boots and set off for Dunston Market.

As he walked along the lane towards the main road, the grey clouds seemed to gather above his head, darkening by the second. Farmer Seddon, one of his neighbours scurried towards him.

'Good morning,' panted Farmer Seddon, cheerfully. 'I shouldn't wander too far this Monday morning, if I was you. There's a storm on the way, for sure. I can read the signs you know. I can read the signs.'

Farmer Grimes frowned. 'Nonsense!' he said. 'If you look to the east the sky is getting lighter. Absolute nonsense.'

'Have it your own way,' replied Farmer Seddon, shrugging his shoulders. 'But the weather's coming from the west and those gathering clouds are storm clouds.' And he wished farmer Grimes a good day and hurried on his way.

Farmer Grimes looked to the sky and decided to take a short cut across the fields. 'Storm on the way,' he muttered to himself. 'Of course there's no storm on the way. But I'll just take a short cut to save a little time.'

He was half way across the field when he noticed Farmer Maden gathering his cows together.

'Good morning to you!' shouted farmer Maden. 'I'm getting the cows into the barn before the storm breaks. They don't like thunder and lightning. If I were you I'd keep to the road this Monday morning. The bottom of the field is like a swamp after all the rain we've had.'

'Thanks for the advice,' grunted Farmer Grimes, 'but I'm in a hurry. I must get some supplies quickly.'

'Please yourself,' replied Farmer Maden, 'but don't say I didn't warn you.'

'Swamp, indeed,' muttered Farmer Grimes, as he made his way down the field. 'Doesn't know what he's talking about!'

He had no sooner spoken than the ground

gave way from beneath him. His feet sank into a squelch of thick brown mud and he found himself up to his knees in cold, dirty water.

'I don't believe it!' stormed the farmer, straining to free himself. 'He could have told me it was this bad!'

It took the angry farmer ten minutes to escape the grasping mud, and even then he left one of his boots behind.

'I'll sue him!' he stormed, as he limped along the road. 'I'll sue him for a new pair of boots!'

Farmer Grimes reached the wooden bridge

22

that crossed the river. He was now just a mile from Dunston market. The storm clouds were gathering and they reflected the farmer's misery.

He was just about to cross the bridge when a cheerful voice greeted him from the other side. Farmer Grimes glanced up to see the Vicar of Dunston waving at him.

'Good morning!' shouted the vicar. 'And a fine Monday morning it is, too! I shouldn't cross the bridge here, though. The timbers are rotten in the middle. If you take my advice you'll walk further down the river to the next bridge. Have a good day?'

'Have a good day, indeed,' muttered the fuming farmer. 'What does he know about bridges!' And he stepped onto the rickety bridge and walked gingerly towards the middle.

There was no problem. The bridge was fine. Farmer Grimes passed the middle of the bridge and stopped to stare down at the fast flowing water. That was his mistake. There was a crack and a groan and the rotten wood gave way beneath his feet. The frightened farmer dropped through the gaping hole and plunged into the raging river. He gasped and he choked as the water threatened to engulf him but he just managed to crawl to the riverbank. A passing trader rushed to his help, pulling the exhausted farmer onto the muddy bank.

'I don't believe it,' panted the farmer. 'I wish I'd never set off for market.'

'Market?' Enquired the trader. 'I hope you don't mean Dunston market because it's not held on a Monday any more. They've changed market day to Friday.'

The farmer's mouth dropped open, his eyes bulged and he let out an agonised groan as the first crack of thunder sounded above his head and the sky was split by a fork of silver lightning.

Prayer: May we never be too proud or stubborn to take advice. As we live our lives, may we turn to those who are more experienced and able to guide us. May we remember that when we need assurance you are always there to turn to. Amen.

Follow up: Ask the children to identify the main people who give them advice in their lives. Who should they turn to if they have a problem at school? Who can help if they need advice out of school?

Discuss what action you should take if you see someone doing something wrong. Are there times when you should give advice even if it is not requested?

Suppose you strongly advise a child or a group of children to stop bullying someone. What should you do if that advice is ignored?

Discuss the concept that you could be given bad advice. You should always listen to advice but you should consider it carefully and make your own judgement. If in doubt - ask someone you really trust.

THE RAINBOW
Theme: Hope

Introduction: Tell the children about something that has really frustrated you recently - it should not be too difficult to think of something if you are a Headteacher or a teacher! Occasionally, everybody has a bad day. Sometimes you feel that the whole world is against you. As you live your lives, you learn to cope with such days. If you do have a bad day the best thing to do is put it behind you and look forward to a better tomorrow.

Kieran had overslept. His mum had shouted upstairs at five minutes to eight as she always did and Kieran had mumbled his usual reply: 'I'm just getting out of bed, mum! I'm putting my socks on!'

In truth, Kieran had pulled the quilt over his head, planning to have a few extra minutes doze time. Twenty minutes later he felt his mum shaking him roughly.

'Will you get up, you lazy boy! You're going to be late for school. It's gone a quarter past eight!'

'Quarter past eight!' stammered Kieran, his eyes straining to open. 'I'm going to be late for school.'

He stumbled into the bathroom and groped for his toothbrush. He squeezed the tube of paste and began to brush furiously. And then he gasped and spat into the bowl. He had picked up the wrong tube. He was brushing his teeth with his sister's Antiseptic Spot Cream.

'I don't believe it!' he gasped, rinsing his mouth with cold water. 'The day can only get better!'

It didn't. Kieran was so late leaving the house that he missed the school bus. It was pouring with rain and Kieran was in such a hurry that he had left home without his coat. He jogged all the way to school. He arrived ten minutes late, out of breath and dripping wet. The other children had already gone in and Kieran had to pass through the main entrance. Children who were late had to report to the office before they went to class. Kieran pressed the entrance button and waited for the secretary to release the automatic door. The buzzer sounded and he pulled at the door, but it would not open.

The wooden door had swollen with the rain and it was sticking. Kieran tucked his homework beneath his arm and put two hands to the door, tugging for all he was worth. The door jerked open and Kieran stumbled backwards, his homework dropping to the soaking wet floor. He stood and looked at the book, wet through and spattered with mud, and he knew that his teacher would hit the roof.

Five minutes later Kieran stood before Mrs. Grant, who stared in disbelief at the soggy exercise book.

'I'm sorry, Miss, but it wasn't my fault,' explained Kieran. 'The door at the front entrance got stuck and I dropped my homework pulling it open.'

'Of course it's your fault,' snapped the angry teacher. 'If you'd arrived at school on time you wouldn't have been using the front entrance, would you?'

'No, Mrs. Grant,' admitted Kieran. 'I'm very sorry.' And he sidled back to his place where he sat for the rest of the morning feeling wet and uncomfortable.

Kieran got into trouble at lunchtime. It was still pouring with rain and the children could not play out. Mrs. Jennings, the lunchtime supervisor, had organised two monitors to fill the water containers ready for the art lesson that afternoon. Kieran was just standing chatting to them when Darren Higson barged past, knocking him sideways. Kieran stumbled into the monitors and the water containers went everywhere, over the art paper, over the floor and over the monitors.

'Kieran! What on earth are you doing?' stormed Mrs. Jennings. 'You shouldn't even be over there! Go and stand out in the hall where you can do no harm!'

'But Miss . . . it wasn't my fault,' began Kieran.

'Don't argue,' insisted Mrs. Jennings. 'Just do as you are told!'

Kieran took a deep breath and walked out of the classroom to stand on his own in the hall.

Later that afternoon Mrs. Grant was telling the children the story of Noah and the Great Flood.

'Very apt,' thought Kieran, as he stared out of the window. The rain had thinned to a drizzle and a few thin rays of sunshine were trying to force their way through the watery clouds. 'I'll need an ark to get home. Everywhere is soaked through.'

He still felt thoroughly miserable. He just wanted the day to end, but something made him listen carefully to the teacher's words.

'Noah and his family had gone through a terrible ordeal,' Mrs. Grant was explaining, 'but God had guided them and he put a rainbow in the sky as a sign of hope and a promise of a better tomorrow.'

Kieran glanced out of the window, and he couldn't believe it! There was a bright rainbow in the sky. It was still drizzling slightly but there was a rainbow, a sign of better things to come.

'And I want you to remember children,' continued Mrs. Grant, and Kieran was sure she was staring straight at him, 'no matter how bad a day you might have had, there is always hope of a better tomorrow.'

Kieran smiled in quiet satisfaction and he promised himself that he would get out of bed on time the next morning.

Prayer: We know, Lord, that life is not always easy. Sometimes we are faced with troubled times or difficult problems. Give us strength and determination to cope with such times for we know that through you we have the promise of a better tomorrow. Amen.

Follow up: Kieran clearly had a bad day but was everything his own fault? Was it his fault that it was raining? Was he really to blame for spilling the water containers? Do you think he acted correctly when he got into trouble at lunchtime?

You may wish to use the story of Noah in a follow up assembly. Before you read the story, ask the children if they know why God sent a great flood to destroy the world.

It is said that there is a pot of gold at the end of a rainbow. What does this mean? Is there really a pot of gold or does it refer to the rainbow being a symbol of hope?

THE LAZY FOX
Theme: Trickery

Introduction: Certain animals, just like people, have a reputation. For example, a lion is reputed to be brave and strong, a monkey is reputed to be agile. Ask the children if they can name an animal that is reputed to be wise. Which animal is reputed to be stupid? Can anyone name an animal that is thought to be cunning? Why is a fox thought to be cunning? Ask the children to listen carefully to the story that follows and make up their own minds as to whether the fox in the story is cunning or just lazy.

There was once a lazy fox who thought that every other animal was stupid. The fox did not believe in hard work. He believed he could get everything he wanted in life through trickery. He woke up one sunny morning feeling very hungry.

'I just fancy a nice fresh chicken for breakfast,' the fox said to himself, 'and I think I know just where to find one.'

The lazy fox slinked out of the wood and crossed a grassy field. He stood on a raised bank and stared across to Farmer Burton's yard. There they were, chickens, dozens of chickens clucking and fussing and pecking around. The fox moved a little closer, keeping close to the ground, and then he stopped and lay down on the soft grass. He let out a pitiful squeal, which the chickens heard at once. Being curious, four large birds flapped towards him, stopping short when they realised it was a fox stretched out on the ground.

'You've got to help me!' pleaded the cunning fox. 'My leg is trapped in a snare and I can't move. You've got to help me.'

The chickens were clearly suspicious but, when the fox let out another pitiful squeal, the largest bird moved forward to investigate.

The fox pounced lightning quick. He had the chicken in his grasp. There was an eruption of feathers. The three remaining birds chased back to the farmyard in fright as the cunning fox carried off his breakfast.

By lunchtime, the lazy fox was once again hungry.

'It's too easy,' he said to himself. 'I wish it was more of a challenge, really.'

The fox left the safety of the wood and strolled back towards the farmyard. As he was crossing the grassy field, he spied a rabbit basking in the warm sunshine. The lazy fox couldn't resist it. He moved a little closer and then collapsed to the ground, letting out a frightened squeal. The rabbit was alerted immediately.

'Help!' shouted the fox. 'You've got to help me! My leg is trapped in a snare. Please release me before the farmer arrives.'

Now the rabbit knew all about snares. His cousin had been snared and it was rumoured that he had ended up in a rabbit pie. He didn't hesitate. He moved forward to help - and the fox pounced on him as quick as a flash.

'These animals are so dumb,' thought the cunning fox. 'There's not one that's a

26

for me. Will they never learn?'

The lazy fox had eaten so well that it was supper time when he next felt hungry. He slinked out of the wood just as the sun was setting and he prowled around by the edge of the trees. Suddenly, he stopped and stared across to the grassy bank. There was a young billy goat grazing contentedly. The fox had never tasted billy goat and he licked his lips in anticipation. He moved forward, once again keeping close to the ground. When he felt he was near enough, he collapsed to the floor and let out an agonised squeal. The billy goat ignored him completely. He didn't even look up. He just kept munching at the grass.

'Strange,' thought the fox. 'It's always worked before. Perhaps he's a little deaf.'

The fox stood up and moved closer. He sunk to the ground and squealed again, this time longer and louder. Still the billy goat did not react.

'Right,' thought the fox, 'if he wont move, I will!' And he sprung to his feet and charged towards the billy goat.

The clever goat waited until the last possible second before lowering his head and tossing the startled fox high into the air. The fox landed with a thump on the ground, just in time to see the young billy goat charging towards him. It was too late. The goat caught him again, tossing him up like an old rag.

Three more times the goat charged and three more times the frightened fox took off. Satisfied that he had seen off the enemy, the goat then left the fox in a crumpled heap on the ground and returned to his own supper.

The bedraggled fox pulled himself slowly to his feet and staggered back towards the safety of the wood.

'That's it!' he muttered to himself, pitifully. 'No more goats ever again, and no more clever tricks!'

Prayer: May we learn, Lord, that trickery is not the way forward in life. We ask that you teach us the difference between right and wrong. May we always treat others with respect and may we work hard to achieve our goals. Amen.

Follow up: A fable is a story that has a moral. The Lazy Fox is a fable as it shows that trickery is not the way forward in life. Perhaps the children could write their own moral fables using the characteristics of another animal to make their points. (E.g. A wise owl, a brave lion etc.).

A follow up assembly could utilise one or more of Aesop's fables. Tell the children something about Aesop and choose appropriate fables to read.

STEPHANIE'S TEST

Theme: Temptation

Introduction: Begin by asking the children if they know what the word 'temptation' means. You may define temptation as 'enticement' to do wrong. Somebody who gives in to temptation knows that they are doing wrong but can not or will not resist. Ask the children if any of them have ever been tempted. (e.g. Has anyone broken a school rule or done something at home that they knew to be wrong?) Choose someone to give an example of temptation. Some forms of temptation may not be too serious - you may be tempted to have an extra chocolate when you have already eaten too many! However, there are times when you may be tempted to do something that you know is really wrong and could possibly lead you into trouble or danger. Can anyone give an example? Sometimes it is very difficult to say no but you must learn to be strong.

Stephanie was nervous. She was not normally a nervous girl but on this particular Monday morning she was really worried. You see, Mrs. Burrows, Stephanie's class teacher, had warned the children that they were going to have a maths test, an important maths test, and she had asked them to take their books home and revise. That had been three weeks ago. Somehow, the time had just disappeared and although Stephanie had taken home her maths books, she certainly had not opened them. She hadn't done one single scrap of revision - and now she was nervous.

It wasn't that Stephanie had not meant to revise. She knew that maths was not her strongest subject and that the test would be difficult. It was just that there were so many other things for her to do - places to visit, friends to see, activities to take part in. On the first weekend, just after Mrs. Burrows had told the children about the maths test, Stephanie had gone to stay with her grandparents. She went quite regularly to her grandparents. They lived some distance away and it meant her staying overnight. Stephanie could have taken her homework with her but somehow it didn't seem worth it.

The second weekend was Saema's party.

Saema was her very best friend and Stephanie had been excited for the whole week leading up to the party. Lots of other people from Stephanie's class were at the party. Saema had even invited some of the boys - but they still had a good time. Stephanie was so tired when she arrived back home that she just flopped on her bed and went straight to sleep, her maths books piled on the bedside table beside her.

This last weekend she had been shopping with her mum. They had set off for the local town centre early in the morning and had spent most of the day there. Mum had even taken Stephanie to her favourite café for a pizza lunch. Stephanie did remember about her maths test when the waitress brought the bill, and she realised that she could have revised during the week but there had been so many good programmes on television and besides, she had felt really tired last week.

Now, as she sat in class waiting for the papers to be given out, Stephanie could feel a sense of growing panic.

'Leave the test paper face down on your desk until I tell you to turn it over,' instructed Mrs. Burrows.

Stephanie sat at the back of the class and she was the last one to receive her test paper. Mrs. Burrows returned to her desk and faced the children.

'Now,' she said, 'there is nothing in this test that we haven't covered in class. If you have done your revision I am sure you will not have a problem.'

Stephanie felt a shiver of apprehension. She stared down at the back of the test paper wishing she were a million miles away.

'Turn over your papers and begin!' Stephanie's hand moved slowly towards the test paper. Her mouth felt dry. She turned it over and began to read the first question - and then she stopped and stared in amazement! She could not believe her eyes! Mrs. Burrows had given her the answer sheet! The questions were there all right - but Mrs. Burrows had pencilled in the answers to every single question! Stephanie sat at the

back of the class; hers had been the last paper given out; Mrs. Burrows must have had the answer sheet on the bottom of the pile!

Stephanie glanced round. All the other children were working quietly, concentrating on their own sheets. She could complete the whole test and nobody would ever know that she had been given the answer sheet. Mrs. Burrows stood silently by her desk, looking round at the children working. Stephanie stared at her for a moment and then she looked back at the test paper. For some reason she felt even more nervous - no, not nervous - uncomfortable. She wrote a number one on her answer paper and prepared to copy out the first question. But she could not do it. Her hand hovered above the paper and she could not write down the question. She put her pencil down and raised her hand into the air.

'Yes, Stephanie? Is there a problem.'

'Please, Mrs. Burrows, I think you've given me the answer paper by mistake!'

The teacher let out a gasp and moved forward to collect Stephanie's paper.

'What an honest girl, Stephanie! How on earth could I have done such a thing! What a good job you weren't tempted!'

Stephanie swallowed hard and waited patiently for a replacement paper that she knew she would not be able to do.

Prayer: Dear Lord, Lead us not into temptation. We often say these words but how often do we think about them? We ask that you guide us and teach us the difference between right and wrong. When we are tempted, give us the strength that we may make the right decision. May we live our lives by following your example. Amen.

Follow up: Temptation is the main theme of the story. However, the first half of the story raises other issues. See if the children can identify these issues (e.g. setting priorities; organising time; not leaving things until the last minute). You may need to give a few clues. Ask the children: 'Do you think Stephanie would have been tempted if she had found time to do her revision?'

Everyone is tempted at some time in life. You may wish to read from The Bible where Jesus was tempted by the Devil (Matt. 4). Explain to the children that it is how you react to temptation that is important. Can the children give examples of temptations that they might have to face as they grow older? (Smoking, drugs, alcohol etc.)

The children could write their own short stories about a character who is tempted in some way. Perhaps some of the stories could be used for a subsequent assembly.

CENTRE STAGE

Theme: Appreciation of music

Introduction: Prior to the assembly, arrange for a couple of the teachers and a few children to bring in a piece of their favourite music. Obviously, you may wish to include yourself. Play excerpts of the music and ask each contributor to say why he or she chose their particular piece. It is likely that you will get a considerable variety, taking in different types of music. Explain that the wonderful thing about music is that there is something to appeal to everyone. It is wonderful to be able to listen to music and it is even more wonderful if you are able to play an instrument yourself.

The girls had practised for months. Lucy, Sam and Jodie had gone over and over their routines until they were absolutely perfect. They had rehearsed every action, every movement and every sound.

Now, as they waited nervously at the side of the stage, the excitement was almost unbearable. As the announcement came over the microphone, they felt a shiver of apprehension. They glanced at each other, smiled and moved forward to take the stage.

It had been Lucy's idea. The three girls had been friends since they were at primary school together. They loved music. They were always talking about the latest bands, singing their songs and practising dance routines in the school playground.

Lucy's mum was a classically trained pianist and she had played in a well-known orchestra for a number of years. Lucy took piano lessons and had reached a very good standard but she wasn't too interested in following in her mother's footsteps, in taking up a classical career. She found pop music much more to her taste, much more exciting and she had found two friends who shared her interest. And so the three girls had got together and called themselves Jade, after the first name of one of their favourite singers.

The other children laughed at them at first - especially the boys. They would stand and mock as the three girls practised their dance routines at lunchtime. They would call them names and mimic them but it had no effect. The girls loved what they were doing and they took no notice whatsoever.

Their very first performance was at the school talent show. The teachers had organised the show for the end of term and the girls, still in Year 5, had been determined to take part. They had practised two numbers for weeks, singing and dancing to a prepared backing tape. They sat patiently at the side of the stage as the other children took their turns. A young boy from Year 3 recited a funny poem. He got one or two of the lines wrong but the audience seemed to like him. Daniel Berry from Year 6 did his ventriloquist act. He did the same thing every year. He had a scrawny looking glove puppet, a bright orange bird with a long neck, and he threw himself all over the stage. The younger children loved it - especially when the puppet attacked the Deputy Head Teacher. Several children mimed to C.D. tracks and one or two tried to tell jokes. They weren't very funny and everybody had heard them before. And then it was Jade's turn. They took their places on the stage, costumes immaculate, confidence high, and the backing track started. What a performance! They sang their hearts out, danced with energy and enthusiasm and they didn't make a single mistake. The audience went mad. Even the boys who had mocked them clapped and cheered and it was clear from the way the teachers glanced at each other, clapping and nodding their heads up and down, that they were really impressed. The girls had felt nothing like it. They were thrilled and their success at the school talent show made them all the more determined to stick together.

It was soon after the talent show that Sam's mum offered to manage them. She had once been a dancing teacher and she recognised that the girls had real talent and the determination to succeed. Of course, she contacted the other parents to make sure that they did not mind. All three sets of parents agreed that the children's schoolwork had to come first but they were keen for the girls to receive good advice and they wanted them to be properly looked after.

Things moved quickly. They had further backing tapes made and they practised more routines. They repeated their success at the school talent show the next year and they started making appearances elsewhere - Summer Fetes, charity concerts, promotional events. Sam's mum made sure that they remained level-headed and, most importantly, the girls got on well themselves. No one thought they were better than anyone else. They worked together as a team and they all shared the limelight. It wasn't long before the local newspaper featured Jade on the Entertainment Page. 'Destined for Stardom,' the report stated. This was followed by an interview on local radio and an offer to record some tracks for a promotional C.D. The girls noticed that none of the boys mocked them now. Just the opposite! Everyone wanted to know them!

And now they stood at the side of the stage, in the wings of the local T.V. studio, waiting for their turn to appear on the T.V. talent show. They had come a long way since that first school performance but they knew that a lot of hard work still lay ahead of them. The announcement came over the microphone. The new all girl group Jade was being introduced to the studio audience. There was that shiver of apprehension as the girls moved forward to take centre stage.

Prayer: We thank you this morning, Lord, for the gift of music. May our minds be broadened by the many different types of music. We thank you for those who compose music, for those who write lyrics and for those who perform. May we learn to appreciate that the love of music can last for a lifetime. Amen.

Follow up: It would be nice if some of the children who are able to play a musical instrument could perform at the end of this assembly. Perhaps there is a recorder group or a school band? If not, there is almost sure to be a confident individual who specialises in a particular musical instrument.

Do a survey with the children to establish current favourite artists. Also, ask the children to conduct a survey with their parents to find out what type of music they like.

Could a group of children develop a simple questionnaire?

PARENTS' EVENING

Theme: Taking pride in what you do

Introduction: Obviously, the assembly is best given prior to a Parents' Evening. Ask the children why they think school organises Parents' Evenings? Explain that it is an opportunity for parents to speak to the teachers and see how their children are progressing at school, both in terms of work and behaviour. Explain that not everyone can be top of the class, the best in everything that they do. What is important is that children work hard, always give their best and behave well. Parents and teachers can not ask for anything more.

Tell the children that for this morning's story they are going to listen to two 'case studies.'

Jordan was not getting on very well at school. He knew it, his parents knew it and his teachers knew it. It was not that Jordan lacked intelligence. In truth, he was a bright boy who learned quickly. The problem was that he was not interested. He did not apply himself to work. He just could not be bothered. As a result, he was always getting into trouble. He would sit and play with his ruler, or jab his pencil into the girl sitting next to him. He would doodle on his workbooks or try to sneak a sweet into his mouth during lesson time. In fact, he would do anything but the one thing he was meant to do - work. It was approaching Parents' Evening and Jordan's books were a disgrace.

'What am I going to say to your parents?' said Mrs. Dunne, in despair after Jordan had produced next to nothing during numeracy. 'I know you can do this work, Jordan, but you just haven't bothered. You've sat and drawn an alien in your book instead of finishing your fractions.'

The other children laughed but they knew it wasn't really funny.

'And what can I tell them about your behaviour?' continued the teacher. She folded her arms and stared at the boy. 'You were in trouble yesterday lunchtime for answering back the dinner ladies. Do you think your parents will be proud of you after Parents' Evening?'

'No, Mrs. Dunne.' Jordan stared at the floor.

'Well you tell me, what are you going to do about it, Jordan?'

'Try harder, Mrs. Dunne.'

'Good,' said the teacher, handing back Jordan's book. 'I hope you really mean it. Now go back to your place and finish your work.'

Jordan strolled back to his desk and immediately started to draw ears on his alien.

Mark had worked really hard at his History Project. He wasn't the brainiest boy in the class but he enjoyed everything about school and he always tried hard. As he stood in the line, waiting for Mrs. Dunne to look at his work, he just knew that she was going to be pleased. One of Mark's best qualities was determination. He never gave up if something seemed too difficult for him. At the beginning of the school year he had been disappointed not to be chosen for the school football team. However, he kept turning up for training and eventually, Mr. Turner had given him a game. He had played so well that Mr. Turner couldn't drop him and he had been a regular ever since.

Mark was just the same with other areas of his schoolwork. He found numeracy difficult and he often had to ask for extra help but he always stuck to his task and he was beginning to make good progress. He enjoyed writing - especially stories - and Mrs. Dunne often chose him to read samples of his work out to the other children. He was so consistent in his attitude to work and in his behaviour that he was popular with everyone in school, teachers and children alike.

'Right, Mark, let me see your work,' said Mrs. Dunne, and she reached out and took hold of Mark's file. The first thing she noticed was the quality of presentation. Mark had taken great care to produce his neatest handwriting and, although he wasn't a brilliant artist, his pictures were accurate and well drawn.

'This is an excellent piece of work,' enthused Mrs. Dunne. 'You've really tried hard, Mark. One or two spelling mistakes to correct - but a beautiful piece of work. I think your parents are going to be very proud of you this evening. You always try your hardest and you take a real pride in your work. What's more, you behave yourself. I never have to talk to you about behaviour, apart from when you chatter a bit too much! Well done, Mark! Keep it up!'

Mark took back his project from Mrs. Dunne and returned to his place to correct his spellings. He felt really pleased with himself and he just knew that his parents would be proud of him.

Three tables away, across the room near the window, Jordan was leaning back on two legs of his chair. He had a wooden ruler in his hand and he was just about to flick a paper pellet across the classroom.

Prayer: Dear Lord, teach us to work hard at school and behave in a reliable and sensible way. Teach us to listen carefully, to take advice and to think for ourselves. Give us the determination to succeed, even when work seems difficult. May we learn to take pride in everything that we do. Amen.

Follow up: Discussion can centre on the two case studies. Ask the children if they think Jordan was happy at school. Why did he behave in such a manner? It was not that Jordan could not do the work, it was that he could not be bothered. Who would be the best person to help Jordan? Would Jordan be a happier person if he achieved more?

Mark was not the cleverest person in the class but he was happy at school. What were some of the good qualities Mark had? (Determination, a hard work ethic, consistency, good behaviour, reliability etc.). Give an example of how determination made Mark's life more enjoyable.

Ask the children to think carefully which of the two children they would rather be like.

MISERABLE MARY

Theme: Enjoying life to the full/Smiling

> **Introduction:** Begin by telling the children that you are going to have a close look at them. Make a show of staring at the children and looking at children in different classes. Choose three or four children who are always smiling to come out and help you. Ask the other children what they notice about the helpers. (Give a clue, if necessary - e.g. Look at their faces.) When you have the answer that they are always smiling, tell the children how good it is to see happy, smiling faces. People who are always smiling cheer everyone up - unlike the girl in the story to follow.

Mary was always miserable. No one ever saw her smile. She was one of those children who lived her life with a permanent frown on her face. In truth, Mary had nothing to be miserable about. She was a very lucky girl. She had parents who cared for her and provided her with all she could ask for. She lived in a lovely house and, although she had an older brother and a younger sister, she had a bedroom all to herself. Her mum and dad smiled, her brother and sister smiled, the other children at school smiled but Mary was always miserable.

'I don't understand it,' said Mary's mum. It was Parents' Evening and she was talking to Mrs. Hargreaves, Mary's teacher. 'The rest of the family isn't like that. We're always laughing and joking but Mary just doesn't seem to join in. She never used to be like that. It's as if she enjoys being miserable.'

'Well, she certainly does not have any problems with her school work,' explained Mrs. Hargreaves. 'She works hard and she is making very good progress - but I have to admit, she doesn't seem to enjoy her work. We can never get a smile out of her?'

'I'm worried,' admitted mum. 'I heard one of her friends call her Miserable Mary the other day. She's not going to have any friends if she doesn't buck her ideas up!'

'We'll see if we can do something about it,' promised Mrs. Hargreaves. 'I can see no reason why Mary shouldn't go round with a big smile on her face.'

The following morning, Mrs. Hargreaves made a point of standing by the classroom door as the children entered. She greeted the children with a friendly 'Good morning!' and got a cheerful reply from most of them. She made a special point of speaking to Mary.

'Good morning, Mary,' she said, smiling pleasantly. 'What a beautiful morning it is, isn't it.'

Mary stared at the teacher, face straight, not a flicker of a smile.

'Lovely,' she said, and walked straight to her table where she slumped down and folded her arms.

'This is going to be hard work,' thought Mrs. Hargreaves, 'but we'll have her smiling by the end of the day?'

At break time, Mrs. Hargreaves asked a few members of the class to remain behind. She chose cheerful children who never had a bad word to say about anyone.

'I want you to help me,' explained the teacher. 'I'm a little bit worried about Mary. She always seems so unhappy. Do you think you could make a big effort to cheer her up? See if you can get her to smile a bit more?'

'That could be difficult,' said Ben Brown. 'I haven't seen her smile for years!'

'Exactly,' said Mrs. Hargreaves. 'Give it a go, will you? See if you can do something about it.'

'We'll try,' said Lisa Potts, 'but she's not very easy to talk to. She just stands on her own in the playground. She doesn't join in with us.'

'Well maybe that's the problem,' said Mrs. Hargreaves, thoughtfully. 'Maybe she's shy and she finds it difficult to mix with other children. I'd really appreciate it if you could help.'

'We'll try,' promised Ben, 'and we'll make sure we talk to her and not just leave her on her own.'

It was too late to do much that break time. Lisa made a point of lining up next to Mary and she tried to chat to her but Mary didn't say much in reply. It was lunchtime when the children made a real effort. Mary was standing on her own against the wall, arms folded, face stern.

'Hi, Mary,' said Ben, as he approached with a group of three or four other children. 'What are you doing?'

'Nothing!' said Mary, and she looked down towards the ground.

'Why don't you come and play with us?' suggested Melissa Martin. 'We're going on the field for a game of rounders.'

'I'm all right,' said Mary suspiciously, and then she looked up and added, 'thank you.'

'Got a joke for you,' said Ben. 'Why did the teacher put the lights on!'

Mary shook her head.

'Because the class was so dim!'

The other children laughed loudly but Mary's face hardly flickered.

'I've got one,' said Lisa. 'What sleeps at the bottom of the sea?'

'Don't know,' said Ben.

'A kipper!'

'A kipper!' Repeated Ben, giggling, and he nudged Mary with his elbow.

The children thought they saw Mary's mouth begin to turn upwards at the corners but she managed to stop the smile just in time.

'My turn,' announced Melissa. 'What can you eat if you go to Paris?'

'Give in,' said Ben. 'Tell us the answer?'

'The Trifle Tower!'

Ben roared with laughter. He over did it a bit, really - especially as he'd heard the joke before. He laughed that much that he fell over and then that set the rest of the children laughing. When Ben stood up the tears were rolling down his cheeks and when he looked at Mary - there was a definite smile on her face. Mary was smiling and Ben thought how nice she looked when she smiled.

The whistle sounded for the end of lunchtime and the children made their way towards their lines, Mary walking with them.

'One more,' said Ben. 'I've got one more. What do elves do after school?'

'I don't know,' said Mary, before anyone else could answer. 'What do elves do after school?'

'Their gnomework!' said Ben, laughing at his own joke. 'They do their gnomework!'

Mary laughed out loud, so much so that one of the lunchtime assistants turned to see who was making all the noise and her mouth dropped open in astonishment when she realised that it was Mary!

As the children entered class, Mrs. Hargreaves was again waiting by the door. She could see immediately that something had changed during lunchtime. Mary was walking in chatting to Ben and Melissa - and she almost had a smile on her face.

'Good afternoon, Mary,' said Mrs. Hargreaves. 'Have you had a good lunchtime?'

'Yes thank you, Mrs. Hargreaves,' said Mary, confidently, walking towards her desk. And then she stopped and turned back to the teacher. 'I've got a joke for you, Miss. What are prehistoric monsters called when they sleep?'

'I don't know,' said Mrs. Hargreaves, taken aback.

'Dinosnores!' said Mary, with a huge smile on her face. 'Do you get it, Miss? Dinosnores!' and she turned round to see that Ben Brown had fallen to the classroom floor in a fit of laughter!

Prayer: Help us, Lord, to appreciate that we have many things in our lives to be happy about. We have families, friends and teachers who care for us; we have books to read, games to play and knowledge to gain. Help us to be cheerful people who enjoy life. May we go about our daily tasks with smiles on our faces. Amen.

Follow up: The story raises several points for further discussion. Mary's mum told Mrs. Hargreaves that Mary had not always been miserable. Can the children suggest what it was that made Mary unhappy? Sometimes, children who appear to be different in some way are treated badly by others. Why does this happen? Discuss what can be done about it.

Reinforce how nice it is to see children (and teachers!) walking around school with smiles on their faces. It makes everyone feel better.

You could finish the assembly by asking the children if they have any jokes of their own!

TEETH OF THE WEEK

Theme: Personal hygiene/dental health

Introduction: Begin by asking a general question: 'Who has been to the dentist recently?' Choose a few children and ask what treatment each child received. Someone is sure to have had a filling. It may be interesting to survey each class, or possibly just the junior classes. Ask the children in Year 3, 'Who has never had a filling?' Progress to Year 4 etc. Ask the children generally why they think fillings are needed and how they can be avoided. Tell the children that their teeth have to last them a long time and it is therefore very important to take proper care of them.

Mrs. Marsden stood in front of her Year 4 class, toothbrush in one hand, tube of toothpaste in the other. She had taken special care to brush her own teeth earlier that morning and she beamed at the children, displaying two rows of perfect white teeth.

'Now then,' she began, 'we are going to start our project about dental health. The very first thing I want you to do is smile at me! Go on - let me see everyone give a great, big toothy grin!'

Mrs. Marsden looked around the class as twenty-nine children grinned back at her. She walked backwards and forwards, staring at individuals before returning to her position in front of her desk.

'Hmmm,' she said, thoughtfully. 'Some of you have lovely, clean white teeth but others, I'm afraid, are not so good. Let me see how many of you have had fillings. Put up your hand if you have ever been to the dentist and had a filling?'

Mrs. Marsden let out a gasp as the majority of her children raised a hand. She counted carefully before announcing, 'Twenty-three of you! Twenty-three children out of twenty-nine have already got at least one filling!

Why do you think that is? Why do so many children need fillings?'

'I think it's because we eat too many sweets,' said Emma Hulse. 'My mum says I should cut down on sweets.'

'Too many sweets,' repeated Mrs. Marsden. 'Most sweets contain a lot of sugar, which is very bad for your teeth. If you have toffees and chewy bars they stick to your teeth and bits stay there for a long time, don't they? And it's not just sweets that are bad for your teeth. Cakes and biscuits and sugary drinks all attack your teeth.'

'My Grandad ate a lot of sweets when he was a young boy,' said Duncan Morris, waving his hand in the air. 'He hasn't got any teeth left now. He has false teeth, Miss. He puts them in a glass at the side of his bed every night. I saw them last week when I went to stay for the night!'

'Yes, thank you, Duncan,' said Mrs. Marsden, frowning in distaste. 'Let's carry on, should we? What else could cause you to need a filling?'

'You might need fillings if you don't brush your teeth properly,' volunteered Dale

Stubbs. 'My mum makes me brush my teeth at least twice a day?'

'Yes, and you have got beautiful teeth,' said Mrs. Marsden. 'I noticed, Dale, that you are one of the children who has never had a filling. It is important to make sure that you don't just brush your teeth but that you brush them properly.'

'My Grandad doesn't have to brush his teeth at all,' interrupted Duncan. 'He puts a special tablet in his glass and it all goes fizzy and cleans his false teeth.'

'Yes, thank you!' snapped Mrs. Marsden. 'I think we've heard enough about your Grandad's false teeth, Duncan. Now, in a few minutes, when we have finished talking, I am going to give each of you a new toothbrush and a tube of toothpaste from this special pack I have received. You may not realise it but there is a correct way to clean your teeth and we are going to practise together. One final thing; while we are working on this project, I think we should have a little competition. I'm going to call it 'Teeth of the Week.' I want you all to make a special effort to look after your teeth. Avoid sugary foods and clean your teeth really thoroughly. At the end of the week we'll have an inspection and I'm going to award a special certificate to the person I think has the Teeth of the Week.'

'Brilliant!' said Duncan, rubbing his hands together. 'I'm going to win that.'

'Well one thing's for sure,' said Mrs. Marsden, smiling at him politely, 'you stand a lot more chance than your Grandad, Duncan!'

Prayer: Help us, Lord, to take good care of ourselves. Make us aware that personal hygiene is important, especially as we grow and mature. We are thinking particularly today about our teeth and of the importance of regular brushing and a healthy diet. May we always appreciate that there is nothing so precious as a smile. Amen.

Follow up: Have a new toothbrush, a tube of toothpaste, a glass of water and a bowl available. Ask for a volunteer to come out and show everyone how to brush his/her teeth properly. (You could prime someone prior to the assembly).

The story identifies food and drink that is bad for teeth. Talk about healthy foods. What type of things are good for teeth? You could use a whiteboard to list things that are good and bad for teeth.

Hold a 'Teeth of the Week' competition!

LIFE BEYOND THE COUCH

Theme: Hobbies

Introduction: Begin by talking about one of your own hobbies. Tell the children when you started your hobby and why you enjoy your hobby. Ask the children about their hobbies, trying to get a selection of different activities. Has anyone got an unusual hobby? Ask why people have hobbies. Explain that a hobby is something that can stay with you for your whole life.

'Why don't you get yourself a hobby?' said Ellen's mum, as she cleared away an empty glass and a crisp packet from a small table that had been placed beside the settee. 'Do something interesting instead of just lying there watching television.'

'I like watching television,' replied Ellen. She flicked the channel so that she wouldn't miss the start of her favourite cartoon. 'Watching television is my hobby. You can learn a lot from television, you know.'

'Not from the programmes you watch,' said mum. 'You'd learn a lot more if you read a book.'

'What's the point?' said Ellen. 'I read a book at school when I have to. I'd much rather watch T.V. than read a stupid story.'

'The point is,' said mum, standing directly in front of the screen, 'that you are becoming a blob - a couch potato. You do nothing but lie there from the moment you arrive home from school to the moment you go to bed. You really should find yourself a hobby!'

Ellen's mum meant what she said. Ellen had always enjoyed watching television but, over the last few months, she had watched it more and more so that the T.V. set in the corner of the room had begun to rule her life. She had even asked for a television in her bedroom when it was her ninth birthday but her mum and dad had refused, causing Ellen to sulk for a week. Ellen's parents were determined that their daughter should break the habit and they decided that drastic action would be necessary.

A few days later, Ellen arrived home from school as usual. She threw her jacket across the back of a chair, dropped her bag on the floor and plonked down on the couch as usual. Ellen reached for the remote control and pressed the stand-by switch. Nothing happened. The television screen remained blank. She pressed again, a little bit harder. Still no response. The television was dead.

'Mum!' shouted Ellen, her face breaking into a deep frown. 'There's something wrong with the T.V.! It won't work.'

'Oh, yes,' said Ellen's mum, walking into the room, 'it went off at lunchtime. I've 'phoned the engineer and he's coming to take it away for repair tomorrow morning.'

'Take it away?' repeated Ellen. She looked horrified. 'He can't take it away. Is he going to leave a replacement?'

'I don't think so,' replied mum. 'He said we should have it back within a week.'

'A week!' exclaimed Ellen. Her eyes were

wide and her face was pale. 'I can't do without the T.V. for a whole week! I'll miss all my favourite programmes.'

'Oh, dear,' said mum, quietly. 'You'll just have to find something else to do, won't you.'

Ellen was not happy. She sulked for two days and she walked around the house with a face that would crack a mirror. On the third day, when she arrived home from school, she went straight up to her room and pulled a book from her shelf. It had been bought as a present the previous Christmas and Ellen had not even bothered to open it. She flicked through the first pages, began to read a little more seriously and was soon engrossed in the story. Ellen's mum put her head around the bedroom door and smiled in satisfaction. Ellen didn't even notice her.

The following morning, Ellen announced over breakfast: 'I've arranged to go swimming with Jane after school. Her mum said she'd take us both and then drop me off at home, if that's all right, mum?'

'Of course it's all right,' said Ellen's mum,

and she added: 'I thought you'd forgotten how to use your arms and legs. It's good to see that there is life beyond the couch!'

When Ellen arrived home later that evening, after she had been swimming, she couldn't stop talking about it.

'It was great!' she enthused. 'It wasn't just ordinary swimming, it was a proper swimming club with real coaches. I wasn't very good really but the coach said I'd get much better with regular practice. It is all right if I join, isn't it mum? I want to go every week.'

'I'd be very pleased if you were to join the swimming club,' replied mum, 'and you can tell Jane's mum that I'll share the transport with her.'

'Brilliant!' said Ellen, and she went straight upstairs to finish her book.

The family was having supper later that evening when Ellen's dad suddenly announced: 'I think I'll bring the television in from the garage now. Your mother tells me you've successfully broken the habit.'

'What do you mean?' said Ellen. Her mouth had dropped open in surprise.

'The television,' repeated dad, 'It's been in the garage for days. I have to admit that we tricked you. The T.V.'s fine! There's not a thing wrong with it.'

'But it wouldn't work,' stammered Ellen. 'It wouldn't even switch on!'

'They won't if you take the batteries out of the remote control,' said dad, and he put his hand into his pocket and pulled out two small batteries which he shook in front of Ellen.

'I don't believe it,' said Ellen. 'How could you? Anyway, you can keep your rotten television! I'm going to be far too busy to watch it.'

'That's what we were hoping,' said mum. 'Life isn't that boring after all, is it, Ellen?'

Prayer: Help us, Lord, to live a full and active life. We cannot be good at everything but we know that everyone is good at something. Give us interest, knowledge and determination to succeed. May we grasp the many opportunities that are presented to us in life. Amen.

Follow up: Ask for volunteers or select a small number of children to prepare and present a short talk about their individual hobbies. The children could bring in pictures or items of interest to illustrate their talks. The talks could firstly be presented in class and then be presented in a follow up assembly.

Alternatively, children from one class could write about their hobbies and the work could be displayed for all to see.

TOO BUSY TO HELP

Theme: Helping others/selfishness

Introduction: Some people give up their lives to help other people. They consciously decide to work with the poor, the sick, the starving or the homeless, even though their own living conditions might not be good and, in some cases, even though their lives may be put at risk. We can not all live our lives that way but we are all faced with situations where we can help others. Sometimes we may only be able to help in a small way - but thinking of other people is a good habit to develop.

A selfish jackal was making his way home through the undergrowth late one evening when he heard a strange hissing noise. He crept forward cautiously and was surprised to see a snake trapped beneath a large branch that had fallen from a tree.

'What are you doing there?' asked the jackal, suspiciously. 'Why don't you slide away?'

'Pleas-s-se help me,' hissed the frightened snake. 'Can't you see I'm s-s-s-stuck.'

The jackal walked around the snake, staring down at him in faint amusement.

'I can't stop now,' he said. 'I'm on my way home for supper. I'm late as it is. Anyway, you shouldn't have got yourself into such a mess in the first place!' And the selfish jackal walked on.

A few minutes later a monkey, playing high in the trees, spotted the unfortunate snake and swung down to help him. The monkey pulled the branch off and the grateful snake was set free. The monkey checked the snake was all right before swinging off towards the swamp for a drink.

A little further towards home, the selfish jackal heard a painful cry, which seemed to be coming from the nearby swamp. He crept

forward to investigate and was surprised to see a monkey stuck fast in the mud at the edge of the swamp. The jackal smiled to see the monkey struggling and sinking ever deeper into the grasping mud.

'Don't just stand there, do something!' implored the desperate monkey. 'Can't you see I'm sinking?'

'I know what you mean,' replied the jackal, nodding his head, 'but what could I do? If I waded in to help you, we'd both be stuck, wouldn't we? Far better for one of us to survive.' And the selfish jackal walked on.

A few minutes later a giraffe wandered down to the swamp for a wade in the water. He saw the poor monkey and rushed forward to help. The giraffe stood on firm ground and stretched his long neck out towards the desperate monkey, who threw his arms around it immediately. Within seconds the monkey was pulled from the swamp and set down on the firm, dry ground. The giraffe checked that the monkey was all right, had a quick drink and then wandered back in amongst the trees to feed on the fresh green leaves.

The jackal had not got much further when he heard a frightened scream coming from amongst the trees. He couldn't resist it. He had to have a look. He crept forward only to be met by a most strange sight. There was a giraffe, his long neck stretched upwards, his head firmly stuck between two branches of a sprawling, leafy tree.

'Get me out!' he gasped. 'Please get me out! Can't you see I'm choking?'

'I don't think it's any time to be joking,' said the jackal, smiling through his thin lips. 'You look in a spot of bother to me.'

'I said choking not joking!' gasped the giraffe. 'Don't waste time - please set me free!'

'Well, that's a little difficult,' explained the selfish jackal. 'I'll tell you what, I'll come back tomorrow and check if you're all right.' And the selfish jackal walked on.

Luckily, the snake, fully recovered from his ordeal beneath the branch, heard the giraffe's cries and he wound his way up the tree to assist the trapped creature. The snake curled around one of the offending branches and pulled it away from the giraffe's neck, allowing the grateful giraffe to free his head.

The snake checked that the giraffe was all right before gliding back down the tree and into the undergrowth.

The selfish jackal was still chuckling about the unfortunate animals he had met when disaster struck. Suddenly, the ground gave away from beneath him and he felt himself falling through space. He landed at the bottom of the pit with a thump that knocked the breath out of him. When he had recovered a little, he realised that he had fallen into a mantrap and there was no way out. He threw back his head and howled for help. He howled and howled and howled until his

throat was so sore that he had to take a rest. He sat down and looked up to the edge of the pit and was delighted to see three inquisitive faces staring back down at him. There was the snake, the monkey and the giraffe, peering over the edge of the pit at the trapped jackal.

'Don't just stand there,' urged the jackal, 'get me out. Can't you see that I'm trapped?'

'S-s-so you are,' hissed the snake. 'S-s-sorry to s-s-see you're s-s-stuck.'

'I've got a problem with pits,' admitted the monkey. 'A cousin of mine was trapped in one and the hunters came back. If you take my advice you'll keep right away from pits.'

'Don't fancy putting my neck down there,' said the giraffe. 'I'd much rather stretch up to the trees.'

The jackal was trembling with fear. He looked from one animal to the other in desperation.

'You've got to help me,' he implored. 'You can't just walk away and leave me.'

'Ah,' said the monkey, 'but that's exactly what you did to each of us. We were all in trouble and you couldn't be bothered to help. What would have happened to us if we hadn't helped each other?'

The jackal looked pitiful. His eyes drooped and his head dropped.

'Of course we'll help you,' said the giraffe. 'If everyone behaved like you our world would be a terrible place.' And he lowered his neck deep into the pit for the jackal to scramble to safety.

'Just remember,' hissed the snake, as the jackal stood shaking at the edge of the pit, 'next time you have the opportunity to help someone - take it.'

The jackal nodded his head in shame and thanked his new found friends for their help.

Prayer: Dear Lord, may we never be too busy to think of other people. Teach us to be kind and considerate people who will always do our best to help others. Help us to understand that being helpful brings its own rewards. Amen.

Follow up: It is very easy to take things for granted, both at home and at school. Ask the children to identify ways in which they could help to make life easier and more enjoyable for their parents and their teachers.

Comparisons can be made with the parable of the Good Samaritan. Remind the children of the parable and ask them about the similarities.

Discuss jobs that involve helping others. Why do people want to become nurses, policemen, social workers etc.?

HONEST JOE
Theme: Honesty

Introduction: Ask the children why they think it is important to attend school regularly. Ask if anyone has been off school ill recently. Choose some children to explain why they were off ill. Explain that sometimes, when you are ill, you have no option but to stay off school. It would not be fair to come into school and pass on your illness to other children or members of staff. However, there are times when you might be feeling just a little off colour, when you have a cold or you are tired but you are still fit to come into school. It is at times like these that you have to be honest with yourself and make the effort to get yourself to school - unlike the boy in the story that follows.

Joe did not particularly like school. It was not that he couldn't do the work. He was a bright boy who had few problems with his lessons. No, it was more that he would just rather stay at home where he could watch T.V. or play on his computer. However, Joe was a normal, healthy ten year old and he had very little time off due to illness - until he discovered a way to get off school without being ill.

The idea came to him one Tuesday afternoon in the middle of an art lesson. Emma Harris, who was working next to Joe, suddenly went very hot and red in the face. She tried to carry on with her picture but after a few moments she raised her hand to attract the teacher's attention.

'Mrs. Jordan, I don't feel very well,' explained Emma, and her voice was quivering.

'Oh, dear, you don't look too good, Emma,' replied the teacher. 'Come and tell me what is wrong with you.'

Within twenty minutes, Emma's mum had arrived to collect her from school and Emma was on her way home. Joe couldn't resist it. He waited another five minutes and then he raised his hand.

'Yes, Joe? What can I do for you,' said Mrs. Jordan.

'Please, Miss, I don't feel very well,' said Joe. He put on the most mournful voice he could muster. 'I've been working next to Emma. I must have caught whatever she's got.'

Mrs. Jordan took off her glasses and stared hard at the boy.

'Well, I must say, you don't look as poorly as Emma, Joe. However, if you are sure you're not well you had better go to the office. We don't want you passing germs around, do we?'

Joe couldn't believe his luck. He couldn't believe how easy it was. The school secretary phoned for his mum and within a quarter of an hour he was on his way home.

Joe's mum was quite concerned at first. She had been at work when she got the phone call and she had come away immediately. She was a little suspicious, however, when after half an hour at home watching television, Joe suddenly asked for a packet of crisps and proceeded to eat the lot within seconds.

'Back to school for you tomorrow,' said Joe's mum. 'You certainly haven't got anything too serious, have you.'

Two days later, Joe tried the same thing again. He knew he had a maths test after morning play and he hadn't done any homework or revision for the test. As the whistle went for the end of playtime, Joe tottered up to Mr. Sanders, the teacher on duty. He clutched his stomach and explained that he had dreadful pains that were making him feel sick. Mr. Sanders wasn't totally convinced but he was so busy supervising the other children that he sent Joe straight to the office. Once again, Joe's mother was called from work and it was not long before Joe was on his way home.

'I hope you really are ill,' said Joe's mum, as they drove the short distance home. 'I can't afford to stay off work every few days, you know.'

'Of course I'm ill,' lied Joe. 'I've got really bad stomach ache and I feel sick.'

However, Joe's mum became even more suspicious when his friends called around after school and Joe declared himself fit to go out for a game of football. In fact, she was so suspicious that she made a phone call to school and had a word with Joe's teacher. When he came in at suppertime, Joe's mum looked at him sternly and said, 'I know what you've been up to, Joe - and so does your

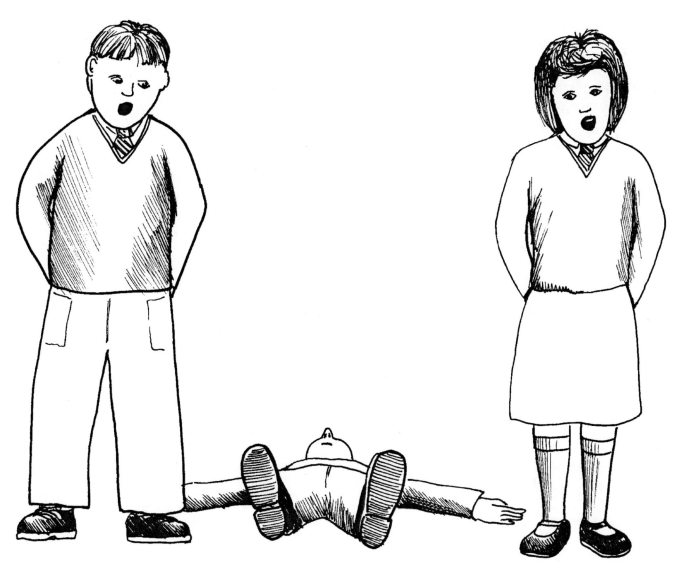

47

teacher! We'll have no more lies, eh? I've told your teacher that you're a very good actor and I think she'll be very suspicious if you claim to be ill again, don't you?'

Joe didn't say a word in reply but he decided there and then that he wouldn't approach the teacher again pretending to be ill. He would just have to think of some other way to get off school.

Joe was in for a shock the following week. He had felt a little odd over the weekend and when he got up to go to school on Monday morning, he could not face his breakfast. He told his mum that he felt sick and was surprised at her response.

'You're going to school,' said mum, firmly. 'A few hard lessons will soon take your mind off it.'

He sat quietly through registration and by the time the children were walking into the school hall for morning assembly, he felt decidedly queasy.

'You look a bit green,' said Emma Hughes, pulling a face at him. 'Don't you think you'd better tell someone? You look like an alien!'

'I - I'll be all right,' said Joe, and his face turned a deeper shade of green.

It was during the hymn that Joe fainted. The children had just begun to sing 'Morning Has Broken' when there was a thud and when everyone looked around, Joe was flat out on the hall floor.

Ten minutes later he was recovering in the school office. His teacher, Mrs. Jordan, was standing by his side holding a glass of water.

'Why didn't you say something?' asked Mrs. Jordan. 'You've always been quick enough in the past to tell people when you haven't felt well.'

'I've lied in the past,' admitted Joe. 'I pretended to be ill just to get off school - but I'll never do it again! I promise I'll never do it again!'

'Have you heard the story about The Boy Who Cried Wolf?' asked Mrs. Jordan.

Joe nodded. Mrs. Jordan didn't say another word - but Joe knew exactly what she meant.

Prayer: Sometimes, Lord, we feel guilty because we know we are doing wrong. Teach us that honesty is the best policy. May we never try to trick or deceive others for our own gain. Give us the strength to tell the truth when we have made mistakes and help us to live our lives as honest and truthful citizens. Amen.

Follow up: Discuss the ending to the story. Check that the children know the story 'The Boy Who Cried Wolf'. What is the moral of both stories?

Ask the children why they think Joe did not tell the teacher when he was really ill. Discuss the concept of 'feeling guilty.'

WIN AT ALL COSTS
Theme: Fair Play

Introduction: The attitude of famous sportsmen and women these days seems to be to win at all costs - either by fair means or foul. The ideals of 'fair play' and 'sportsmanship' seem to have faded into the background. It is said that professional footballers, for example, spend time practising how to dive in order to trick the referee. An opposing player only has to come near them in the penalty area and they throw themselves to the ground. I am sure you can think of a few well-known players who have a reputation for diving. Of course, people play sports and games to win but surely, if you know you've won by cheating and not because you are genuinely better than the opposition, that win is devalued.

Carl was absolutely mad about football. It was all he ever thought about. His bedroom was covered with posters of his favourite players and he even had a quilt and pillow bought from the souvenir shop of the local football club. All of his spare time was spent either playing or watching football. In fairness, he practised hard and worked at his skills. As a result, he had reached a very high standard for a boy who was just ten years old.

Carl played a few games for the school team when he had been in Year 5 and, now that he was in the top class, he was a regular choice. In fact, Carl was the leading scorer. He played in attack and he had a knack of being in the right place at the right time. He had already scored twenty goals in the current season. His teacher, Mr. Jackson, said he was 'a natural'.

Clough Street Primary School was having an excellent season. They were second in the local primary school league and they had reached the final of the knockout cup. Unfortunately, they had to play Manor Road, their bitter rivals and the one team who were above them in the league.

Mr. Jackson had spent a lot of time throughout the season training the team and, as the day of the big match approached, he organised one final after school training session. The practice went well. The boys worked really hard and they felt fit and sharp.

'We're in with a great chance,' said Mr. Jackson, as the boys changed back into their school clothes. 'If you play like that tomorrow evening, the cup will be ours.'

'Don't worry, Sir,' said Carl, cheerfully, 'I've been practising my diving. I'll win at least one penalty.'

The smile disappeared from Mr. Jackson's face. He looked horrified.

'I hope that was a joke, Carl,' he said sternly. 'If I thought you'd cheated to win a penalty I'd have you off that field straight away. There would be a substitute on in seconds.'

'But sir - everyone does it!' chipped in Barry Parker, Carl's best friend. 'Even the professionals practise diving!'

'Everyone doesn't do it!' snapped Mr. Jackson. 'We don't do it. If we can't win fairly I'd rather not win at all. I want to win that cup because we are the best team - not because we are the best cheats!' And he turned his back on the boys and walked out of the room.

The referee started the match promptly. A slight drizzle was falling but conditions were good. The first ten minutes were really even with neither team taking control. Gradually, however, Manor Road began to dominate. A superb cross from the right wing was met by their centre forward and his powerful header thudded against an upright before being cleared up the field. Two minutes later, that same centre forward, a big fair-haired lad called Wesley Higgs, burst through the Clough Street defence and bore down on goal. Clough Street's centre back put in a last ditch tackle and won the ball cleanly. But Wesley Higgs had other ideas. He let out a piercing yell and threw himself convincingly to the ground, rolling over twice before clutching his leg.

The referee did not hesitate. He blew his whistle and pointed to the penalty spot. Carl couldn't believe it. The centre forward had taken a dive. He had clearly taken a dive!

The referee ignored all protests and Wesley Higgs himself, having made a miraculous recovery, strolled up to take the penalty. There was a hushed silence. The whistle blew and Wesley struck the ball. It flew past the goalkeeper's despairing dive and settled in the back of the net. Wesley raised his arms in the air and the Manor Road supporters went wild.

At half time, before Mr. Jackson could say a word, Carl vented his anger.

'He cheated! He took a dive! Everyone could see it!' protested Carl. 'Everyone but the ref., that is!'

'Surely you don't blame him for that?' said Mr. Jackson. 'After all, Carl, you've been practising your diving haven't you?'

Carl didn't reply. He looked ashamed. He'd learnt the hard way how unfair it is to cheat.

Mr. Jackson turned towards the team and said, 'Now then, you're not going to let a goal like that rob you of the cup, are you? Get back out there and put some pressure on them. If you're determined enough, you can still do it.'

The second half was fantastic. Both teams battled away as the rain came down heavier and conditions worsened. Manor Road almost increased their lead but Ashley Moor, the Clough Street keeper pulled off a great save, and then he saw a gap up field and he lofted the ball towards Carl. One touch from Carl put Barry Parker into space and his first time shot rocketed into the back of the net. Clough Street had levelled the score! Their supporters went mad! Mr. Jackson leapt into the air, slipped on the mud and landed on his bottom.

There were three minutes to go and Clough Street, spurred on by the goal, were piling on the pressure. Carl had seen much more of the ball in the second half. His confidence was high. A pass from midfield found him in possession again. He turned like lightning and slipped his defender. He was inside the penalty area and in sight of goal. He drew back his foot to shoot when a sliding tackle from a second defender caught him. He lurched forward and stumbled. He could have gone down. It would have been a penalty - but Carl kept his balance and lashed in a vicious shot. The ball crashed into the back of the net and the game was won.

Two minutes later, Carl held the cup aloft as the crowd clapped and cheered. He grinned at Mr. Jackson, who was standing by his side.

'I didn't go down, Mr. Jackson,' said Carl. 'We won it fair and square.'

'Yes, we won it fair and square,' agreed Mr. Jackson, proudly, 'and doesn't it feel good!'

Prayer: Help us, Lord, to work hard and play fairly. Teach us to be competitive in life in a fair and honest way. May we learn that winning and succeeding in life is only an achievement if it is gained through practice, hard work and honest endeavour. Show us that we cannot always win in life but we can always do our best. Amen.

Follow up: Discuss why it is that some people cheat. Why do some people try to cheat in exams? Is it because they are too lazy to work for their exams or because they are afraid to fail? Make the point that if people cheat they are really only cheating themselves.

Why do people cheat in sport? Discuss the notion that the amount of money at stake has encouraged people to cheat in order to win at all costs.

TOO BIG FOR HER BOOTS

Theme: The importance of staying level headed

Introduction: Have you noticed how some people seem to think they are better than everyone else is?

You often see it with people who become famous - footballers, pop stars etc. You also often find that such people make a mess of their lives because they don't know how to handle fame and the wealth and publicity that comes with it. However, it is not only rich and famous people who think they're something special; it happens amongst ordinary people and even amongst school children. Take care - if you become very good at something make sure that it doesn't go to your head.

Carly was thirteen years old and she really believed that she was a star. She started to change as soon as she was told that she had passed the audition and, by the time she had finished recording the series of seven programmes, she was unbearable.

Carly had done all the right things since she was about three years old. She had gone regularly to Dancing School and had achieved distinctions in all of her exams; she had taken part in Dancing Shows and had got used to performing in front of an audience; and then, when she was just seven, she had enrolled for Drama Classes, where the teacher soon recognised her potential. At this stage it was just a hobby and it was only a few years later, when Carly had moved on to High School, that she realised she could make a career out of acting. She was a popular, pretty girl with a good personality and she had lots of friends - but all that changed after the recording.

'I don't know what's happened to you,' said Lisa Clark, Carly's best friend. 'It's as if you're looking down on all your old   friends since you've got yourself on television. Are we not good enough for you anymore?'

Lisa had a point. Carly had been snooty and flippant and, when her friends had asked her about her T.V. work, she had answered, condescendingly, 'You wouldn't understand. It's not worth explaining to you.'

As a result, Carly found that the friends she'd had for years didn't want to know her. She kept herself to herself and walked around school as if she was something special.

Mrs. Harris, Carly's form teacher, also noticed a change. Carly had always been so pleasant and hard working. She had always contributed to class discussions and she was never late handing in her homework. Now she just sat slumped over her desk at the back of the class and she seemed to have such a superior look on her face.

Mrs. Harris put up with it for a few days and then she asked Carly to remain behind in class when all the other children had been dismissed.

'What is the matter with you?' asked Mrs. Harris. 'I thought you'd come back full of news. I thought you'd be so enthusiastic that you'd be bursting to tell us all about your experiences. You've hardly said a word since you've returned to school.'

Carly shrugged her shoulders and said, 'I just think I'm wasting my time at school. I don't need to be here. Everyone's always told me that I need to work hard and get qualifications if I want to get on in life. Well, that's not true, is it Miss? I've got on in life already. I'm not like the others. They're going to be recording a second series soon and they're writing to me next week with the details.'

'I'm really sorry you feel like that,' said Mrs. Harris, in exasperation. 'I think recording a T.V. programme has gone to your head. You've got too big for your boots. Just remember, young lady - pride comes before a fall.'

It was a whole week before Mrs. Harris next spoke to Carly. She would not have bothered but she noticed that Carly had stayed in her seat at the back of the class after the others had left. Carly was holding her head in her hands and she seemed to be upset.

Mrs. Harris walked over to her and said kindly, 'What's the matter, Carly? What is it that's bothering you.'

Carly raised her eyes. They were red. She had obviously been crying.

'I got the letter from the T.V. Company,' she said, and she sniffed and wiped away a few tears with the back of her hand.

'They don't want me for the next series. They said I'd done very well but my character had been written out for the next series. I haven't told anyone. I feel so stupid.'

Mrs. Harris thought for a moment before saying: 'You've got to put it down to experience, Carly. You've learnt a lot from what has happened - and I don't just mean from appearing on television. Provided you learn from your mistakes you'll be a stronger person for it.'

'I'm sorry,' said Carly. 'That letter has brought me back to earth. You did warn me that pride comes before a fall! Next time - if there is a next time - I promise I'll keep my feet firmly on the ground.'

Prayer: Help us, Lord, to work hard and do our very best in life. We all want to experience success but teach us to be proud of our achievements without becoming boastful or conceited. May we never forget to be kind and considerate to all those around us. Amen.

Follow up: Discuss the concept of 'ambition.' Is it a good thing to be ambitious? What ambitions do the children have and how do they think they can be achieved?

What do the children see themselves doing in ten, twenty, thirty year's time?

MY BROTHER

Theme: Family Life

Introduction: Ask the children if any of the children have a brother or sister who annoys them. There should be a huge response! Ask what sort of things their brothers or sisters do to annoy. Listen to and discuss responses. You may wish to tell the children about some of your own expcriences.

It is always nice to see older children looking after their younger brothers or sisters - taking care of them when they first start school, walking them home, supporting them on Sports Day etc. Family life can be frustrating but it is also very rewarding.

I want to tell you about my brother Liam. The first thing I want you to know is that Liam is really annoying. I mean really annoying. You see, Liam is three years younger than I am and he always seems to get his own way. It was alright until he came along. I used to get all the attention but now I just have to get on with things. Liam seems to have mum and dad wrapped around his little finger.

I'll give you some examples. Whenever we want to watch something on T.V. all Liam has to do is whinge to mum and he gets what he wants.

'Your brother's younger than you,' says mum, as if I didn't know. 'You can't expect him to watch a programme he doesn't understand.'

The minute mum leaves the room he has a silly grin on his face and he sticks his tongue out at me. Really annoying!

He even seems to determine what we eat for the week. Our Liam's a real fussy eater. He doesn't like vegetables and doesn't like chicken - all he seems to like is fish fingers and pizza. I'm sick of fish fingers and pizza. We seem to have fish fingers about three times a week. When I grow up I never want to see another fish finger in my life.

The other annoying thing about Liam is that he thinks he's really funny. He's seven years old but he acts as if he's four. I was having a cup of tea the other evening and I just went out of the room to get a magazine. While I was away he tipped half the salt cellar into my drink. Well, I came back in, picked up my cup and took a big gulp. It was awful! It nearly made me sick! I spluttered everywhere and then got into trouble from dad for making a mess. Our Liam was collapsed in laughter on the floor. He was laughing that much he was crying. Stupid boy!

And then a few night ago I had the fright of my life. I have to share a room with Liam, worst luck. I was getting ready for bed. I threw the covers back and sat down on my bed - and then I saw it. A huge, hairy black spider crawling towards me over the white sheet. I let out a scream and ran from the room. I just stood on the landing, shaking. Of course, I could hear my brother howling with laughter and I knew at once who'd put it there. He's made me a nervous wreck. I check my bed every night now before I get in. Last night he'd left a great plastic tarantula in my bed. I got hold of it and threw it out of the window. Liam went whinging to mum and guess who got into trouble?

A few weeks ago, Liam was getting bullied at school. He didn't say a thing to anyone. To be honest, it was nothing too serious but I knew something was wrong. He wasn't getting up to his silly tricks and he wasn't laughing the same. He seemed to be worried and had a serious look on his face. He even asked if he could walk to school with me. Our school is only around the corner from where we live. We don't even have to cross any roads and Liam usually runs ahead on his own.

Well, this particular morning we were just going through the school gate when he grabbed hold of my arm. I could see two older boys standing just inside the gate and they started calling names and teasing him. At first, I told him to ignore them but I could see he was upset. He told me they were always doing it, even if they saw him walking around school. I was tempted to go and flatten them but Mrs. Gregg, our Headteacher, says we should never take the law into our own hands. Anyway, I went inside with Liam and I spoke to Mrs. Fitton, Liam's teacher. She promised to sort it out that same morning and Liam looked a lot happier.

'Thanks, sis,' he said, and he gave me a big hug. Our Liam actually gave me a hug!

That night Liam seemed much better. Mrs. Fitton had dealt with the two boys and she had told Liam that she wanted to know if there were any further problems. We had fish fingers for tea, he watched all the programmes he wanted, and, when we went to bed, there was that big plastic tarantula on my pillow. Still, I didn't mind - I knew he was back to normal.

Prayer: We thank you this morning, Lord, for our families and for all the love and joy that they bring to us. As we grow up, may we learn to appreciate the value of family life and always play our part in a sharing, caring family. Amen.

Follow up: Teachers need to be sensitive when discussing family life but the following activity should be relevant to all circumstances.

Ask the children to write about one member of their family (include grandparents). They can give some factual information but should concentrate on qualities and characteristics. A picture could complement the work. Selected work could be presented in a follow up assembly.

Discuss ways in which the school community is like a big family. For it to work in harmony there has to be discipline, commitment and co-operation. Just as parents care for children, all those who work in school want to do their best for the children in their care.

WALK TO SCHOOL DAY

Theme: Looking after the environment/Personal health

> **Introduction:** This is an ideal assembly to use if you are planning your own 'Walk to School Day'. Begin with a survey. Ask the children: 'How many of you regularly walk to school? How many come to school in a car? How many of you use public transport?'
>
> In a typical school, these days most children are delivered by car. It might be interesting to explore the reason why. Some children may live too far away to walk to school. Mothers may drop children off on their way to work - but for some it is just a way of life to use the car.

Leeside Primary School had organised a 'Walk to School Day'. Everyone was to be involved; the teachers, the welfare staff, the secretary, the caretaker, the dinner ladies and, of course, the children. They had chosen Friday 12th April and all of those involved were hoping for a dry day.

The week leading up to 'Walk to School Day' was not too promising. It rained every day but, thankfully, the weather started to improve on Thursday afternoon and by Friday morning it was bright and sunny.

'Thank goodness,' muttered Mr. Hopkins, as he drew back his bedroom curtains. 'I didn't fancy getting soaked through before 9 o'clock.'

Mr. Hopkins lived over three miles away from school and it had not been his idea to organise a 'Walk to School Day.' In fact, Lauren Shaw from Year 6 thought of the idea. Mrs. Brierley's Year 6 class had been doing a topic about the environment and, as part of their work, they had been discussing the potential harm caused by car emissions. There were 32 children in Year 6 and 20 of them came to school by car every day, even though most lived well within walking distance. Lauren and her friend, Alison, approached Mrs. Brierley and suggested a 'Walk to School Day' as a way of doing something practical to help protect the environment.

'I think it's a splendid idea,' said the teacher, 'but you will have to go and speak to Mr. Hopkins.'

The Headteacher was just as enthusiastic and the date was pencilled into his diary that very same day. Lauren and Alison drafted a letter, with a little help from Mr. Brierley, for all the children to take home and the day was organised.

Now that the 12th April had arrived, Mr. Hopkins was up bright and early to make the three-mile walk to school. Not everyone was able to walk all the way to school. One or two of the staff lived a considerable distance away and Paul Harris, a Year 5 pupil, had moved house right across to the other side of town. However, they agreed to use public transport to get as close to school as possible so that they could walk from the nearest bus stop. Mr. Hopkins packed his brief case and set off at twenty minutes to eight. It was a lovely morning. He set off at a brisk pace and he had plenty of time to think about the day ahead.

By eight thirty, Mr. Hopkins had arrived at the school gates and he was amazed to see dozens of other children already on their way along the road towards school. They walked in twos, in threes or in small groups and in the next twenty minutes or so, many more arrived by foot, the younger children accompanied by their mothers. Lauren and Alison stood at the gates to greet them as they arrived at school. They had made a big sign out of card that had the words 'Thank You For Walking to School' printed in large colourful letters. Not everyone came by foot. It just was not possible for one or two families to organise. However, there were so few cars arriving outside school that the usual morning traffic jam just did not happen.

School assembly was presented by Year 6 that morning and, of course, the theme was protecting the environment. The Year 6 children explained to the rest of the school how car emissions were damaging the environment and how much healthier the air we breathe would be if emissions were cut. They also explained the benefits of walking instead of travelling everywhere by car. Towards the end of assembly, Lauren asked the children how many of them had enjoyed walking to school and nearly every hand shot up into the air.

When Year 6 had finished their presentation, Mr. Hopkins got up to thank them.

'You know,' he began, 'I really enjoyed my walk to school this morning. I know the lovely weather helped but I think I'm going to try and walk to school far more often. It would be nice to think that some of you will make the same effort. After all, we should all do our bit to help the environment. Let us see if we can make as many days as possible a 'Walk to School Day'.'

Prayer: Help us, Lord, to do all we can to protect the wonderful world that you have made. Make us aware that looking after our environment is for the benefit of all. Teach us the need for responsibility. Small contributions add up and can make a difference to the way in which we live our lives. Amen.

Follow up: Organise a 'Walk to School Day' of your own. Could a group of Year 6 children draft a letter explaining the reasons for holding such a day. Other children could design posters promoting environmental awareness.

Get the children to look critically at the school environment. Is there litter, graffiti, an area that needs improving? Ask the children to write down ways in which they would like to see the school environment improved.

THE ICE DRAGON

Theme: Never judge people by appearance alone

Introduction: It is easy to look at somebody and jump to the wrong conclusion about them. Someone who appears to be stern and fierce might turn out to be really kind and thoughtful. Alternatively, I am sure you know that you should always be wary of strangers who try to befriend you. It is said that actions speak louder than words and this morning's story is about a creature that looked fierce but really only wanted to be friendly.

The ice dragon lived in a dark cave deep in the cold woods a couple of kilometres from the village. She had lived there for one hundred years, all alone in the frozen woods. The villagers would not go near the woods - they did their hunting elsewhere, in the fields or on the hills that bordered the far side of the village. They would warn their children to stay away from the dangerous woods where the ice dragon prowled and the terrified children obeyed their parents.

'She'll breathe fire and scorch you to cinders,' they warned, and the wide eyed children shook with fear. 'She'll capture you and carry you back to her cave,' they would say. 'You will never be seen again!'

In truth, the ice dragon was lonely. She did look fierce, pale green, scaly skin and spiky back and she did breathe fire - but she only used it to keep herself warm, to melt the drifts of snow and the slabs of ice that blocked the entrance to her cave. She had never attacked anyone in her life and certainly had no intention of harming the villagers.

The ice dragon craved company and, after one hundred years, she decided that if the villagers would not come into the woods then she would have to venture out and visit the villagers.

It was bitterly cold. The woods were icy white and thin flakes of snow were falling gently. The ice dragon moved quickly but cautiously, occasionally brushing the trees, dislodging a shower of powdery snow. She reached the edge of the white woods and stared out across the frozen fields towards the village. Everywhere was still. Everywhere was quiet. The snow was still falling. There wasn't a soul in sight. The ice dragon moved forward, slowly but deliberately.

A high, wooden fence surrounded the village and the strong double gates were closed. The gates were always kept closed, especially at night in case the ice dragon came when the villagers were least expecting her.

They saw her before she got anywhere near the gates. There was always somebody on guard and the ice dragon was spotted and the alarm raised. The gates burst open and the villagers poured out. They were shouting and screaming and they waved sticks and hurled stones towards the ice dragon. The ice dragon stood there for a few moments, puzzled and bewildered. Her nostrils flared and steamy white smoke billowed into the cold air. The baying crowd moved forward and one of the stones hit the ice dragon on the shoulder, making her roar with pain, a roar so loud that the villagers backed away in fear. The ice dragon turned and lumbered back towards the safety of the white woods.

The ice dragon did not understand. Seven days had passed and she had not ventured out of her cave since the attack. Why had they chased her off? Why had they waved sticks and hurled stones. The ice dragon did not understand.

The weather had worsened. The wind had increased until it howled through the woods and the snow had turned into a blizzard. It had raged for nearly a week and the entrance to the ice dragon's cave was blocked. Everywhere was frozen solid. The ice dragon had to get out. She needed food. She stood back from the entrance and blew her fiery breath towards the packed snow and ice. The flames roared from her nostrils and within seconds the entrance was breached. She stood in the frozen wood and stared in wonder. She had never seen such snow. It had drifted and frozen, had turned to ice that was as hard as stone.

And then she thought of the villagers. If she was trapped in her cave then the villagers were sure to be in trouble. How would they

59

hunt? How would they feed themselves? The ice dragon made up her mind - she would return to the village to see if she could help. Even though they had attacked her she would return to the village.

The journey was difficult. The snow had drifted and the ice dragon had to battle her way though to the edge of the woods. She moved forward towards the wooden gates and once again she was spotted immediately. The villagers gathered on the platform above the gates but they did not wave sticks or throw stones. They were tired and they were hungry and they just watched as the ice dragon got closer and closer. There was no way out of the village. The snow had piled up against the gates and there was no way out. The ice dragon let out a gentle roar and breathed her fire in the direction of the gates. There was a blast of flame and the snow began to melt, to fall away from the frozen village gates. Another blast of flame and another and another - and the gates were clear. Still the villagers watched in silence as slowly, the ice dragon turned and headed back towards the woods. And then there was a cheer. The gates burst open and the villagers rushed out, shouting and cheering. The ice dragon turned and stared towards them and then she turned again and continued her journey back towards the frozen white woods.

Prayer: Dear Lord, help us to accept people for what they are and not for what they seem to be. We know that looks and first impressions can be deceptive. May we learn to judge people by their actions and by the way that they live their daily lives. Amen.

Follow up: Discuss the story in more detail. Why did the villagers warn their children to keep away from the woods? How do you think people feel who have few friends? Why did the ice dragon decide to help the villagers even though they had been cruel to her? What do you think might have happened after the end of the story?

Draw a picture or make a collage of the ice dragon.

Remind the children how they should react if a stranger ever approaches them.

NOT SO TOUGH

Theme: Fear/ Being sensitive to the feelings of others

Introduction: Explain to the children that nearly everyone is afraid of something. You may wish to tell the children if you have a fear of your own. Ask other teachers present what they are afraid of. This should encourage the children to discuss their own fears. Are there any common fears? e.g. Fear of the dark? Some fears are irrational and have to be faced e.g. fear of the dentist. People should never laugh or make fun of others who are afraid - they should encourage them to try to overcome their fears.

Jake was the biggest boy in his Year 6 class. He looked a year older than most of the other children. He wasn't really a bad lad but he was always boasting about how tough he was. He was a central defender in the school team and it was not often that anyone got past him. He was the best swimmer in his class and he had come first in two races at the local swimming gala. He was a powerful and fast runner and he had represented the school at the town athletics meeting. Jake was good at most physical activities but the trouble was - he knew it and he never missed an opportunity to boast about his achievements. To make matters worse, he could not tolerate the idea that other children could not match up to him in some way, or displayed their emotions openly. Jake thought that anyone who baulked at an activity was 'soft' and he never failed to tell them.

One morning in the summer term there was a fire drill in school. The children filed out of class quickly and efficiently and assembled quietly in their classes towards the back of the playground. Jake noticed that a new boy in Year 3 was crying and he was quick to draw attention to the child.

'Look at him!' mocked Jake, pointing towards the distressed child. 'What a softie! Fancy crying just because we're having a fire drill!'

Jake's teacher, Mrs. Richards, heard the comment and tackled Jake immediately.

'That boy is new to the school,' explained the teacher. 'He only joined us yesterday and he doesn't really know anyone. He probably doesn't even know his way around school yet. He might have thought it was a real fire. I think you should be a little bit more understanding, Jake.'

Jake said nothing but he wasn't convinced.

That same lunchtime a wasp got into the dining room. The dinner ladies told everyone to keep calm and ignore it but some of the younger children made a fuss and panic. Of course, the wasp reacted badly and Amy Jenkins from Year 1 was stung on the arm. She shouted out in pain and the tears streamed down her cheeks.

'It's pathetic,' scoffed Jake, stuffing a whole potato into his mouth. 'I was stung last year and I didn't start crying!'

Mrs. Hatch, one of the dinner ladies, overheard the comment.

'Yes, well you're such a big lump you probably didn't feel a thing!' she said. 'Where there's no sense there's no feeling!'

Jake scowled and shoved another potato into his mouth.

The following day was Friday - the day Year 6 went for their swimming lessons. Jake loved going to the baths. He could show off to all the rest of the children. Two Year 6 girls, Joanne and Leslie, had only just learnt to swim. They were practising going backwards and forwards across the pool with plenty of encouragement from the instructor.

Jake couldn't resist it. He swam towards them and shouted, 'Still in the shallow end, are we? Too frightened to go any deeper?'

The instructor was furious. The girls had been doing really well but they were clearly upset by Jake's comments.

'Leave them alone and get back to the other end of the pool!' snapped the instructor. 'They may be going across the pool but they've made more progress than you, Jake.'

Jake just smiled and glided effortlessly back towards the deep end.

It was later that term when the Year 6 class went on the school adventure holiday that Jake really learnt his lesson. Everything was fine at first and Jake was doing his best to show off as usual. He did really well at the water sports' events. He managed the sailing boat with ease and he was so powerful in the canoe that his boat got to the end of the course well ahead of all the others. The instructors were impressed and they praised him for his strength.

Jake just shrugged his shoulders and said, 'It's easy. There's nothing to it.'

However, on the final afternoon it was the turn of Jake's group to go abseiling. There was a wooden tower in the grounds of the centre and the platform was reached by climbing a series of ladders. Jake took one look at the huge tower and his legs turned to jelly. His knees went wobbly at the very thought of climbing the tower.

The children were strapped into their harnesses and they sat down on a wooden bench near the base of the tower.

'Right, who's first?' asked the instructor.

'How about Jake?' suggested Mrs. Richards. She had noticed that Jake's face had turned pale green.

'No, it's all right,' said Jake, quickly. 'I'll let someone else go first.'

'That's very kind of you,' said Mrs. Richards, and she did her best to disguise a knowing smile.

One by one the children took their turn at abseiling. Not everyone found it easy and the instructors, Mrs. Richards and the rest of the group offered plenty of encouragement. Eventually, there was only Jake left.

'Come on, then,' said the instructor. 'I bet you can't wait to get up that tower!'

Jake pulled himself reluctantly to his feet and made his way to the bottom ladder. He climbed slowly to the first platform. His legs were shaking and his mouth felt dry. He climbed the final two ladders and edged out onto the platform - but he could go no further.

'I can't do it!' he stammered. 'I don't like it! I'm scared of heights!'

The children below were astonished - but not one of them laughed. No one said a word.

'Are you sure?' asked the instructor, kindly.

'It's easy once you go over the edge.'

'Over the edge!' repeated Jake, and he shook even more. 'No fear! I'm going back down!'

Ten minutes later the children were walking back to base with their equipment. Jake had recovered a little and he was next to Mrs. Richards.

'Why didn't they laugh?' he asked, and he was genuinely puzzled. 'I thought they'd love to see me in trouble?'

Mrs. Richards smiled.

'Everyone's afraid of something, Jake. Perhaps next time you see someone frightened or upset you'll have a little more sympathy.'

There's a good chance of that,' said Jake, quietly. There's a really good chance of that.'

Prayer: As we grow and mature, help us, Lord, to be kind and considerate people who are sensitive to the feelings of others. It is natural for us all to be afraid of something.

Help us to overcome our own fears and offer encouragement and understanding to those around us. Amen.

Follow up: Make a list of all the things children say they are afraid of. Use this as the basis for the discussion about fear. What is the one thing that most frightens people? If you talk openly about your fear does it help you to overcome it?

Some people like to be afraid. They go on scary rides, read frightening books or watch a scary film. Why do you think this is?

The children could write group poems about some of the things that scare them.

MRS. OGDEN'S CHILDHOOD

Theme: Appreciation of the way we live today

Introduction: Explain to the children that over the past hundred years life has changed greatly. Being a child in the first decade of the new century is very different from being a child during the first decade of the last century. Ask the children what they do when they get home after school and during the evening. They are bound to mention watching television and playing on computers. Technological advances have changed the world and it is difficult for today's children to imagine what life was like for their grandparents.

Miss Jevons stood before her Year 6 class in readiness to introduce the afternoon's visitor.

'Now then, children,' she began. 'As you know, we are going to continue with our history topic, Britain since 1930, and I have brought in a very special visitor this afternoon.' She turned to the elderly lady who was sitting on a chair next to the teacher's desk. 'This is Mrs. Hughes,' continued the teacher, 'and I know her very well because she is my grandmother. I've asked her to come in and talk all about her childhood in the 1930's and I want you all to sit and listen very carefully. When she has finished talking to you I am sure she will be willing to answer any questions you might have.

Miss Jevons moved to one side and Mrs. Hughes stood up and looked at the children a little nervously.

'Well,' she began, 'the world I was brought up in as a child in the 1930's was very different from the world you know today. The whole pace of life was different - much slower. I'll tell you about my home, first of all. I lived with my family in a small terraced house on the outskirts of Manchester. There were five of us altogether, my mum and dad, my older sister Annie and my brother Harry. Harry was two years younger than I was and he was a right nuisance. We only had two bedrooms so mum and dad had one and us three children shared the other. Harry hated it! He couldn't understand why he had to share with two horrible girls!

I remember the house was freezing in winter. We had no central heating, of course. We had a coal fire like the rest of the street. I can remember waking up on winter mornings and seeing the frost patterns on the bedroom window. It was that cold you could see your breath even though you were inside the house. You children don't know how lucky you are to have central heating! My dad worked at the local factory and he had to be up at 6 o'clock every morning. Before he went off to work he would light the fire so that it had a chance to warm up before we went down stairs.

I can remember we used to play on the rug in front of the fire. We didn't have fitted carpets like most of today's houses; we had a big square rug in the middle of the room. We had a fireguard around the grate but sometimes the coal fire would crackle and sparks would jump out onto the rug. I can remember it smouldering several times.

We had simple toys and games - none of these electronic games you children use today. We played Ludo and Snakes and Ladders and I had a favourite doll called Bessie.

I can see our kitchen now - nothing like today's fitted kitchens with all their fancy gadgets. It was a working kitchen. There were red tiles on the floor and white tiles on the walls. We had an old gas cooker that we had to light with a spill. We always seemed to have a kettle of water on the boil for a cup of tea. My mum didn't have a washing machine or a tumble drier; she had a tub and a mangle to squeeze the water out of the clothes. Wash day was every Monday. The whole street did their washing on a Monday. You could look along the backs of the houses and see lines full of washing. If it was raining all the washing would be dried in the kitchen on a wooden maiden.

Mrs. Ogden paused for a moment, as if she was deep in thought. The children sat quietly and waited for her to continue.

'I could tell you a lot more about home life,'

she said, ' but I'm sure you'd like to know what school was like. I went to Bridge Street School, which was about five minutes walk from our house. Everybody walked to school in those days. Nobody came by car. I wonder how many of you walk to school each morning? Our Head Master was called Mr. Parry and I can tell you he was really strict. He was a tall man with grey hair and a moustache to match. I can remember we all had to stand up every time he walked into a classroom. Even the teachers seemed to be scared of Mr. Parry! He had a cane, of course, and every so often he would carry it around school with him or bring it in to morning assembly just to remind the pupils of its existence.'

'There were over forty children in my class. We all had a wooden desk of our own and we sat in rows arranged in alphabetical order. When we were working we just did not talk. Teacher would patrol around the room making sure we kept to task. I can remember getting into trouble when I was your age, in the top class. I was recovering from a cold and I couldn't stop coughing. Mrs. Lunt, the teacher, told me to control myself as I was disturbing the other children. Of course, as soon as she said it I wanted to cough even more and she thought I was doing it deliberately. She sent me to see Mr. Parry and he made me stand outside his room in the cold corridor for the rest of the afternoon. I was freezing by home time and I became so ill I was off school for a week.'

'I'm going to stop, now,' said Mrs. Hughes. 'I hope I've given you some idea about what it was like to be a child in the 1930's - and thank you all for listening so well.'

Mrs. Hughes sat down. There was a brief pause and then the children in Year 6 gave her a huge clap as a way of saying thank you for such an interesting talk.

Prayer: Dear Lord, we thank you this morning for all of the inventions and discoveries that have helped to make our world more comfortable. We thank you for advances made in medicine and in technology and communications. Help us to appreciate the wonderful world in which we live and never just to take things for granted. Amen.

Follow up: Make a list of things that families have available today that make life easier or more comfortable e.g. washing machine, deep freezer, telephone (and mobile phone!), cars etc.

Ask the children to research other aspects of life in the 1930's - transport, leisure, education.

Discuss the idea that not everything has changed for the best. In the story, Mrs. Ogden suggested that life was lived at a slower pace in the 1930's What did she mean by this?

BARE TREES FARM

Theme: Evacuation/Appreciation of the way we live today

Introduction: Set the scene for the story by explaining that at the beginning of the Second World War many city children had to leave their homes and their families and go and live in the country with host families. This was known as evacuation and the children were evacuees. It was necessary because German planes bombed large cities and ports, such as London, Birmingham and Liverpool. It is hard to imagine what it must have been like. Listening to the accounts of evacuees makes us realise how lucky we are today.

My name is George Dawson and I want to tell you about my evacuation from Liverpool in September 1939.

I was only just seven years old at the time and I didn't really understand what was going on. Oh, my mum had told me that there was going to be a war and I knew that my dad had gone away to join the R.A.F. but it didn't really mean a lot to me.

The problem was that it all happened so quickly. One evening we were having supper in the kitchen when mum started to explain to me and our Sophie that we would be going to stay with some people in the country for a while. She kept saying, 'It's for the best! It's for the best!' but when I asked her who they were and where they lived she couldn't tell me. I knew there was something wrong because she started crying. She tried to hide the tears but I knew she was crying. Sophie was only five and as soon as she saw mum crying she started herself.

The next morning, mum had two small cases packed. She walked to school with us and, when we arrived in the playground, I was amazed to see that all the other kids had bags or cases as well. Mum gave us both a hug and a kiss and then rushed off. I knew she was crying again and I was beginning to feel really worried.

At about 11 o'clock we all lined up in the playground with our cases. I can remember I had a brown label with my name and address on and it was attached to my coat. We all had to carry our gas masks and Mr. Roberts, our teacher, checked that we had them before we set off to the station. Mr. Roberts was brilliant. He was really strict but he had us all singing as we made our way to the railway station. I can still remember the words to 'Run, Rabbit, Run' to this day. It was chaotic at the station. There were lots of other schools there and the platform was crammed with children. Eventually, the train pulled in and we all piled on board. I had a feeling of panic. I didn't know where I was going or when I would be returning home. To make matters worse, I saw our Sophie getting into the next carriage and her eyes were streaming with tears. There was a blast of steam that enveloped the whole platform and the train set off, slowly at first and then gathering speed as it pulled away from the station.

The journey seemed to go on forever. Looking back, it must have only taken an hour and a half but it was the longest hour and a half of my life. I wasn't a soft kid but I really wanted my mum.

Before long, the factories and the houses disappeared and were replaced by trees and green fields. The animals fascinated me. I'd only ever seen pictures of cows and sheep and I hadn't realised that cows were so big. Eventually, the train pulled in at a small, country station and we all got off. There was a long table at one end of the platform and we had to form a queue and wait for our names to be called. It seemed to take ages. Mr. Roberts explained that we were being allocated to our 'host families'. I hadn't a clue what a 'host family' was and I didn't really care by this stage. All of a sudden, when there were hardly any children left on the platform, a severe looking lady called out our names: 'George and Sophie Simpson!' Mr. Roberts pushed us forward and she snapped out, 'You're at Bare Trees Farm.'

'Please, Miss, I don't know where that is,' I said, weakly.

'You soon will do,' replied the severe lady.

'You're with me! I'm your host - and you two ragamuffins had better behave yourselves!'

I have to tell you that her bark was worse than her bite. Her name was Mrs. Grogan and she lived with her farmer husband, Arthur, just a couple of miles from the station. Bare Trees Farm was fantastic. I don't know to this day why it was called Bare Trees because it was surrounded by trees, beautiful trees that turned the most amazing colours as late summer drifted into autumn.

The Grogans didn't have any children of their own and they really looked after us well. We each had a room of our own and they gave us huge meals. Mrs. Grogan said we looked like a couple of scrawny chickens that needed feeding up. We missed our mum and our school friends but I think we were the lucky ones.

Prayer: Help us, Lord, to appreciate our homes and our families. We know we are lucky to have shelter, good food and people who love and care for us. We realise, also, that there are many in this world who are less fortunate. May we never forget the plight of those in need and may we do all we can to help provide for them. Amen.

Follow up: The children could imagine they were evacuees and write about their experiences. Encourage them to write about their feelings, from when they first left home to their arrival at a host family.

The children could do their own research about evacuees. Perhaps this could be set as a challenge for them to do at home.

Talk about the many ways in which life has changed since the Second World War - especially with regard to technology and communications.

AS STUBBORN AS A MULE

Theme: Kindness

Introduction: Ask the children to name someone they consider to be kind. In what way is the named person kind? It is sometimes said that you have to be cruel to be kind. What does this mean? Can anyone give an example? You may give an example where a teacher has to take strong action in order to prevent a child from getting into trouble. Being kind is not always giving away physical things - money, gifts etc. It is being aware of the needs of others.

Brian was a faithful mule who had served his cruel master for years. He worked on a farm five miles outside the bustling town and Burgess, the farmer, had driven him hard, worked him for all he was worth. For years Brian had pulled the cart up and down the fields; he had dragged the farmer's heavy load to market; he had lived in a damp shelter next to the barn and he had been fed on vegetable heads and stubble from the fields. He had never complained because he knew no different. Brian thought that this was how all mules lived. He believed that all mules were born to be treated badly.

Over the past few months things had got even worse. Brian was growing old and he had not got the strength or the stamina that he used to have. He couldn't walk as fast and he had to keep stopping for a rest. Farmer Burgess was growing old as well and, as he grew older, he grew less and less patient.

'Get a move on, you stupid mule!' He would say, and he would clout Brian with a stick in an effort to speed him up.

It had no effect. Brian could be very stubborn and every time Burgess used his stick Brian would slow down a little more.

'If you go any slower,' stormed Burgess, 'you'll come to a dead stop!'

One cold October day Farmer Burgess was returning from town after selling his cartload of harvest vegetables. He was in a particularly bad mood. The wind was howling, a cold rain was beginning to fall and the farmer had got a poor price for his crop. Brian was struggling against the wind, pulling the cart slowly along the track, stopping every so often to catch his breath.

'Hurry up, you useless lump!' shouted the farmer, and his stick crashed down on the mule's back.

The blow stung Brian and he stopped in his tracks as he felt the pain.

'Did you hear me?' yelled the farmer. 'Get a move on, you dumb animal!'

Burgess swung the stick again and it stung into Brian's back. It was more than he could take. He'd had enough. He gave a loud Eye-ore! And stood absolutely still in his tracks.

Farmer Burgess was furious. His face turned beetroot red with rage and he used his stick again. It made no difference. Brian had made his mind up - he was not going to move. The rain came down heavier and the wind blew harder and colder but the mule stood his ground.

Burgess got down from the cart and walked round to face the mule.

'I don't believe it!' he stormed, staring straight into Brian's face. 'How could you be so ungrateful after all these years!'

Brian snorted and stared straight ahead.

The Farmer went back to his cart and picked up an old carrot. He broke it in half and stood just in front of Brian, tempting him to move forward. Brian snorted again and stood his ground. Burgess was dripping wet and hopping mad. He climbed back on his cart and swung his stick again in anger, catching Brian a glancing blow that made him wince with pain. Instinctively, Brian kicked out with his back legs, causing the cart to veer upwards. Farmer Burgess let out a yell and tumbled from his seat. He crashed to the ground and landed in a puddle lined with thick mud. He was furious!

At that moment, another cart appeared on the road, pulled by a young, healthy looking mule with a fine coat. It was farmer Gregson, one of Burgess's neighbours. The cart pulled alongside the filthy farmer, who was still sitting in the puddle, shaking with rage.

'Oh dear, oh dear,' said farmer Gregson, shaking his head. 'What on earth has happened to you?'

'Ungrateful creature!' stormed the farmer. 'Threw me off my cart. After all I've done for that mule!'

Farmer Gregson looked at Brian and noticed the marks on his back. He saw how thin the old mule looked and how poor his coat appeared.

'All you've done for him?' repeated Gregson, and he dismounted and stroked Brian on the nose. 'I've seen you going backwards and forwards to market for years. I've seen how you treat your mule - or should I say mistreat. You don't deserve a faithful creature like this. You're not fit to look after an animal!'

'Is that so?' yelled Burgess. He tried to get up but fell back into the mud. 'Well if you think he's so wonderful you take him! You look after him - if you can get him to move, that is?'

'It will be a pleasure!' said Farmer Gregson, and he unfastened the harness from Brian's shoulders.

The mule stepped forward immediately as Farmer Gregson stroked his nose. Burgess scowled and clenched his fists.

'A little bit of kindness never hurt anyone,' said Farmer Gregson, and he walked off down the road with two mules and a cart leaving the angry old farmer sitting in the mud with the cold rain still falling.

Prayer: Teach us, Lord, to be kind and considerate people. May we always put the needs of others first and never say or do anything that could hurt or upset those around us. Help us to live our lives to the full by following your example. Amen.

Follow up: Set the children a challenge 'to be kind.' Can they be kind and helpful at home? Can they be kind and helpful at school? Tell them that the teachers are going to be watching and listening for acts of kindness over the next few days. Perhaps each teacher could nominate a particularly kind and helpful pupil to be recognised in an end of week assembly.

THE TRAINING SHOE

Theme: Making the most of the talents you have

Introduction: Name some celebrities who have a special talent and ask the children what they are well known for doing (e.g. a footballer, a pop star, an author etc.). Even though these people have great talent, they have probably still had to work hard to realise that talent. A talented footballer has to build up a level of fitness; a talented musician has to practise. Not everyone can be famous but everyone should try to make the most of the talents they have.

Sarah found schoolwork difficult. It was not that she didn't work hard - if anything, she worked harder than most of the other children in her class. It was just that subjects such as literacy, numeracy and science did not come easy to her. She would, for example, take her spellings home every Monday and spend all week learning them in readiness for the spelling test on Friday morning but she had never yet got full marks. In fairness, her teacher, Mrs. Thomas, knew that Sarah always tried her best and she did her utmost to encourage her.

'It doesn't matter,' she would say, quietly, when the other children had gone out to play. 'As long as you continue to do your best that's all anyone can ask of you.'

'I do try,' explained Sarah, 'I just find work difficult. I'm not very good at anything, really. I can't play a musical instrument and I don't think I'm going to get in the netball team.'

'Of course you're good at something,' said Mrs. Thomas. 'It can take a long time to discover your talent but it's there, hidden away, just waiting to break free!'

Sarah was not convinced but she smiled politely and followed the other children out into the playground.

That afternoon Sarah's class was having an art lesson. The children had been wondering why Mrs. Thomas had asked them to bring in a training shoe. Mrs. Thomas got the children to arrange two or three trainers in the centre of each group of tables and explained that they were not to be moved. Special drawing pencils were given out. They were brand new. The children hadn't used them before. Mrs. Thomas told the children that the best artists were keen observers who paid attention to the smallest detail. She showed them how to use their pencils to ensure that angles and lines were accurate and how to hold them when they wished to shade a particular area and then she set the children to work.

Sarah had always enjoyed drawing but she had never really worked with just a pencil, trying to create a detailed observational sketch. She used her pencil faintly to begin with, putting in the main lines to ensure correct shape. She seemed to get the perspective right at once and she strengthened the lines to give a firm outline.

Mrs. Thomas, who had been walking around the tables giving help and advice, stopped and looked in admiration at Sarah's work.

'That looks terrific,' said the teacher, and she held it up for the rest of the children to see. 'A really promising start, Sarah.'

Sarah beamed with pleasure and concentrated even harder. Her picture got better and better as she filled in the intricate detail and added shading. By the time she had finished she was really pleased with herself.

Mrs. Thomas held up the completed picture for the rest of the class to see.

'Sarah, I'm not going to put your work up with the rest of the pictures,' said Mrs. Thomas. 'I think it deserves to go on display in the school entrance area.'

At the very end of the afternoon Mrs. Thomas kept Sarah back for a few minutes.

'Do you remember what I said to you earlier?' Asked the teacher. 'You know - about everyone having a talent, even if it remains hidden for a long time.'

Sarah nodded and smiled.

'Well, it didn't take long for us to discover your talent, did it, Sarah? You make sure you practise it and develop it - you owe that to yourself.'

Prayer: We know, Lord, that we cannot be good at everything. Help us to work hard and always try our best. Give us the determination to develop the talents that you have provided and teach us to always treat others with the respect they deserve. Amen.

Follow up: Ask the children what they think the teacher meant when she told Sarah that she 'owed it to herself' to develop her talent for drawing.

When people grow up they often say that they wished they had persevered with something they used to do - e.g. playing a musical instrument, learning a foreign language etc. Discuss the point that giving up on something too easily and too early can mean missed opportunities.

It might be interesting to ask a class to do Mrs. Thomas's art lesson. It would be interesting to see some of the results in a subsequent assembly. Could one special picture be chosen to go on display in the school entrance area?

THE BENEFIT OF THE DOUBT

Theme: Patience and understanding/Learning not to react badly

Introduction: Ask the children if they know what it means to give someone 'the benefit of the doubt.' Explain that in a court of law a person accused of committing a crime is innocent until proved guilty. It is up to the prosecution to prove the case and the members of the jury should only convict the accused if they have no doubt about his/her guilt. This does not always happen in everyday life. Sometimes people are too quick to react when they think they have been wronged and, as a result, mistakes can be made.

Daryl Higgs was in Year 6 and he was not a pleasant boy. In fact, he was a bully and, to make matters worse, he had a very short temper. He was constantly getting into trouble for picking on the younger children and his parents had been called into school to see Mrs. Sharp, the Headteacher, on several occasions. It didn't seem to make any difference. Daryl seemed to think that he had a right to pick on the younger children and he could not understand why people made such a fuss. Daryl thought that he was always right and that everyone else was wrong. He did not have many real friends but a couple of the other Year 6 children hung around with him because they were frightened of him.

One morning playtime Daryl was standing in the middle of the yard talking to Jamie Hughes. Some of the Year 5 children were playing football but Daryl insisted on standing right in the middle of their pitch. The ball had already hit him on the head and he had turned round and scowled in the direction it had come from. A few minutes later, Paul Mason chased a long goal kick and ran straight into the back of Daryl. He hadn't done it deliberately. He had been watching the ball and he just didn't see Daryl. The two boys crashed to the ground, Paul landing right on top of a startled Daryl Higgs. Daryl was furious. He lost his temper immediately. He lashed out with his arm and he caught Paul full in the face with his elbow. Paul yelled out in pain and clutched at his face immediately.

Mrs. Thomas, the teacher on duty, had seen it all happen and she was on the spot in seconds.

'Daryl Higgs!' she stormed. 'What on earth do you think you're doing? How dare you lash out like that! Do you not realise the damage you can do?'

'He started it!' protested Daryl, getting to his feet. 'He knocked me over first.'

'Yes, but it was an accident,' said Mrs. Thomas. Paul was just getting up from the floor. He already had a large bruise beneath his right eye. 'I saw it all happen. You didn't even give him a chance to apologise. You lashed out at him without giving him the benefit of the doubt. I want you to go and stand outside Mrs. Sharp's room and don't you ever do that again!'

'It's not fair!' muttered Daryl, as he made his way across the yard. 'He ran into me first and I'm the one who gets punished!'

The next incident happened that same lunchtime. Daryl had just collected his tray from the hatch and he was walking over to his place at the dining table. Unfortunately, someone had dropped a blob of mashed potato on the floor. Daryl stood on it and his foot slid forward at once. He tottered for a moment and then completely lost his balance. His feet went from under him, his dinner tray flew up into the air and he crashed to the floor. To make matters worse, he had flailed out with his arms and caught the drinks trolley as he fell. A full jug of orange juice and several glasses were knocked over. Daryl just sat there in a pool of orange juice with a blob of mashed potato on his head.

Mrs. Thomas had witnessed the whole incident. She walked across to the embarrassed boy and stood over him.

'Daryl Higgs!' she said, seriously. 'You deliberately knocked over that drinks trolley. I saw you do it.'

Daryl was astounded. 'I didn't, Miss!' he protested. 'I just slipped on the floor. I couldn't stop myself from falling. It was an accident, Mrs. Thomas, honestly!'

'Oh, it was an accident?' repeated Mrs. Thomas, and her face softened a little.

'You didn't mean to do it - just like Paul didn't mean to run into you and knock you over in the playground.'

Daryl was beginning to understand. He looked really sorry for himself.

'I'll tell you what I'm going to do,' said Mrs. Thomas. 'I'm going to give you the benefit of the doubt. However, next time someone bumps into you or even knocks you over I expect you to do exactly the same. Now go to the washroom and clean yourself up. You look really ridiculous!'

IF I ONLY HAD A LITTLE MORE

Theme: Laziness and Greed

Introduction: Ask the children if any of them know what they want to be when they grow up. Ask questions such as: Why do you want to be a footballer? pop star? dancer? etc. Ask, 'What do you think you will have to do if you are to achieve your ambition?' The answer, of course, is work hard. Explain to the children that they will never achieve anything if they are lazy. Ask the children to listen carefully, for the main character in the story to follow was not only lazy, he was also very greedy.

Goran was a trickster. He would travel the countryside with his mule begging whatever he could from the people he met. It wasn't that Goran was poor. Far from it. He lived in a large farmhouse and he had land of his own, left to him when his father had died some years ago. Goran was, however, lazy - very lazy indeed. The farm building, which had once been the best for miles around, was dirty and in disrepair and the once rich land was overgrown with grasping weeds and brambles.

'Why should I slave away on the land?' reasoned Goran. 'If people are stupid enough to give me things for nothing, then I am grateful enough to accept.'

And so he went out begging. In truth, he looked like a beggar, for he took no pride in his appearance. His hair was long and straggly and his beard was ragged; his coat was torn and dirty and the clothes he wore beneath looked as though they had been rescued from a scarecrow. His boots were thin and worn and they let in the rain so that his feet were permanently wet. Even other beggars used to keep away from Goran. The more Goran begged and the more people gave him, the greedier he became.

One cold, wet day Goran was out on the roads with his mule. They had travelled some distance and the mule was tired, for he had not been fed for days. Goran spied a farmer working his fields and, as he approached, Goran could see that he was digging up potatoes.

'Could you spare a few potatoes for a poor, unfortunate man?' pleaded Goran, leaning over the farmer's gate.

'Of course I can,' replied the farmer, seeing the state of Goran's clothes. He filled a sack full of potatoes and passed it over the gate.

Goran hoisted the sack onto the mule's back without so much as a 'thank you' and, just as he was about to leave, he turned to the farmer and said, 'Oh, and if I only had a few carrots what a nourishing stew I could make!'

The trusting farmer fetched a bag of carrots and Goran smiled to himself as he made his way down the road.

It wasn't far to the next farm, where Goran came across a large man loading onions onto a cart.

'Could you spare a few small onions for a poor, unfortunate man?' said Goran.

He made his voice tremble, as if he was starving.

'Of course I can,' replied the generous farmer, and he filled a sack full of his best onions.

Goran loaded the sack onto the mule's back, who sagged under the weight.

'Oh,' continued Goran, 'and if I only had a few turnips what a nourishing stew I could make!'

The trusting farmer fetched a bag of turnips and Goran grinned to himself as he made his way down the road - a little more slowly, as the poor mule was struggling.

It wasn't long before Goran came across a busy farmyard. A dog, which was barking, strained to break free from a rope that was attached to a wall. Chickens ran loose, pecking at the farmyard floor and flapping in fright. The farmer's wife was packing some long, green, beans into boxes, ready to store for the winter. She looked a little startled as Goran approached, dragging the tired mule behind him.

'Good day to you,' said Goran, pleasantly. 'I see you've had a good harvest of beans. I wonder could you spare a few for a poor, unfortunate man?'

The farmer's wife glanced at the sacks and bags weighing down the mule but she was a kindly lady and she passed over a box of beans, which Goran accepted at once.

'Oh,' he said, as he balanced the box on the mule's back, 'and if only I had a nice round cabbage what a nourishing stew I could make!'

The farmer's wife duly found him a cabbage and Goran turned to go without giving any thanks.

'Oh,' he said, as a frantic chicken pecked at the ground near his feet, 'a couple of nice chickens would keep me going for weeks!'

The farmer's wife just wanted to get rid of him so she agreed that Goran could take a couple of chickens and she sighed with relief as he left the farmyard, the poor mule wobbling behind him.

'Time I replaced you!' grumbled Goran, pulling at the mule's rope. 'I could do with finding a farmer who has a spare mule!'

It was getting late in the day and Goran decided to head for home. He had begged enough food to last him for weeks but he was still in a bad mood. The poor mule was really struggling, tired, hungry and weighed down with sacks and bags. Even the two chickens rode on the mule's back. Goran and the mule had just climbed a steep hill when they came to a dead stop on a rickety wooden bridge. The mule was so weak it could not take a step further.

'What have you stopped for, you dumb animal?' Goran whacked the mule with a stout stick. 'Get a move on! It will be getting dark!'

The mule winced with pain and stared straight ahead. Goran whacked it again, even harder, and the mule lurched forward, slipping on the rickety bridge. Goran let out a yell as the mule stumbled to its knees, throwing the sacks, the bags, the box of beans and even the two chickens off its back and in to the fast flowing river beneath.

'You stupid creature!' raged Goran, and he leaned over the side of the bridge to rescue what he could. 'A full day's work wasted! All wasted!'

Goran leaned further over the bridge as the wobbly mule tried to stand up. It staggered slowly to its feet, lurched sideways and knocked Goran over the bridge and into the cold, swirling water below. Goran thrashed and spluttered as he struggled to the riverbank. He had lost everything and, if anyone had seen the mule, standing on the bridge, staring down at his dripping wet master, dirty, dishevelled and miserable, they would have told you that it had a definite smile on its face.

Prayer: Dear Lord, sometimes we are greedy and take more than we really need. It is easy to forget those who do not have enough food or adequate shelter. It is hard for us to imagine what it must be like to be really hungry. Help us to play our part by caring and by sharing what we have. Amen.

Follow up: There are several issues in the story that merit discussion. Goran was clearly lazy and very greedy. The people he met, however, were kind and giving. Were they too trusting? Should they have given food to Goran without question? How might they have dealt with Goran?

The story could be continued. What might happen next? Does the poor mule suffer because of Goran's anger? Has it the strength to run off? Does somebody else appear on the scene and rescue the mule?

If the story is used near harvest time, discuss the fact that many people in the world are starving even though there is enough food produced in the world for everyone. Why are some people starving while others have plenty? People of the world need to learn how to share more effectively. Talk about organisations that help those in need.

JOANNE'S DINNER MONEY

Theme: Temptation

Introduction: Begin by asking the children if they know what it means to be tempted. Ask if anyone has ever been tempted to do something wrong. Some of the examples given may not be too serious. Explain to the children that sometimes, being tempted to do wrong could lead to danger - e.g. being tempted to climb on the school roof. Also, giving in to temptation could lead you on to do more serious things. It is sometimes difficult to say 'no' if you are with a group of friends who tempt you to do wrong. It takes a great deal of courage and strength.

I'll tell you how it happened. It was first thing on Monday morning and I was a little late arriving in class. Mrs. Tucker was already taking registration and I just got to my place as she called out my name. I hadn't had a good start to the day. Monday was Games day at school and I couldn't find my trainers. Mum went mad. She'd only bought them for me the week before and she'd made me promise to look after them. I know I'm careless but I don't lose things on purpose. I was convinced I'd put them in my school bag but when I came to look, they just weren't there! Mum made me promise to look for them at school. She said I'd have to pay for a new pair myself if I couldn't find them. That's why I was late in class. I spent five minutes looking in the cloakroom and when there was no sign of them there I rooted through the Lost Property Box. They had to be somewhere. They wouldn't just run off on their own.

Anyway, I shoved my school bag underneath my table - and that's when I saw it. It was a brown envelope and I knew at once that it was a dinner money envelope. I don't know what made me do it but I put my foot over it straight away and just sat there as Mrs. Tucker finished the register.

It was then that Joanne Hughes put her hand up. Joanne sat in front of me and she was a real pain. I knew what she was going to say even before she opened her mouth.

'Please, Mrs. Tucker, I've lost my dinner money. I know I put it in my bag when I came out to school.'

'Go and check the cloakroom,' replied Mrs. Tucker. 'See if you've left it in your coat pocket.'

I should have said something, I know I should - but I just kept my foot over the envelope and watched as Joanne left the class and made her way towards the cloakroom. I don't know what made me do it. I felt guilty straight away. I suppose it was the thought of having to pay for a new pair of trainers. It would be weeks before I could save enough to replace the ones missing and I wouldn't be able to afford anything else in the meantime. Still, I knew I was doing wrong by not saying anything and I felt really strange.

Joanne came back in and she was almost in tears.

'It's not there, Mrs. Tucker. I'm sure I brought it in to class with me. It was in a brown envelope and it had my name on it.'

'Don't worry,' said Mrs. Tucker, kindly, 'we'll have a search for it. I'm sure it will

78

turn up if you say you brought it into class.'

She turned to face the rest of us and said, 'Has anyone seen a brown envelope containing Joanne's dinner money? Will you all have a good look in your trays and on the floor.'

I suddenly felt worse than ever. Everyone was searching for Joanne's envelope and it was underneath my foot. I began to feel hot and I was sure my face was turning red. I ducked below my table and picked up the envelope.

'I've got it, Mrs. Tucker,' I said, and I waved the brown dinner money envelope in the air.

'Well done, Daniel,' said Mrs. Tucker. 'It's nice to know we've got such honest children in this class.

'Thanks, Daniel,' said Joanne Hughes.

'My mum would have made me pay if I'd lost my dinner money. Thanks very much.'

I should have felt better - but I didn't. All right, I made the right decision in the end but I shouldn't have even had to think about it. Funnily enough, I found my trainers later that day. I'd left them in the changing room after P.E. What a good job no one was tempted to take them.

Prayer: Dear Lord, there are times when we are tempted to do wrong. Sometimes it is hard to say 'no'. Give us the courage to do what we know is right. Help us to follow your example and live our lives in an honest and truthful way. Amen.

Follow up: Why did Daniel put his foot over the dinner money envelope? What was it that made Daniel give the dinner money back? Daniel was pleased that no one had stolen his trainers yet he had considered stealing Joanne's dinner money. Ask the children what they think about Daniel. Discuss the concept of 'conscience'. Ask the children if any of them have had a 'guilty conscience' because they know they have done something wrong. Reinforce the message that sometimes a great deal of strength is needed to say 'no' and to do the right thing.

A BRAND NEW BABY

Theme: Family Life at Christmas/Remembering the birth of Jesus

Introduction: Begin by asking the children what it is they like about Christmas. You will probably be given answers such as receiving presents, Christmas dinner, a holiday from school etc. Take time to discuss their answers and develop as appropriate. Ask why it is that we have a holiday at Christmas? Explain that if a very special baby boy had not been born more than 2000 years ago there would be no such thing as Christmas. It is always exciting when there is a birth in the family but this was a birth that changed people's lives forever.

It was the 20th December, the last day of the school term and just five days before Christmas. All the exciting activities that had taken place at St. Luke's School were now over. The Christmas plays had been more successful than ever and the children had enjoyed their Christmas parties, but now they were finished for another year. It was the last day of term and it was 'Toy Day'.

Hannah was in Year 3. She had brought in last year's Christmas Doll and mid way through the morning, Mrs. Wright, her class teacher, saw Hannah sitting quietly on her own in the corner of the classroom. She was holding her doll as if it were a real baby but she did not look happy.

'Whatever's the matter, Hannah,' said Mrs. Wright, sounding concerned. 'Why aren't you playing with your friends?'

'I don't want Christmas this year,' replied Hannah, a single tear appearing in her eye. 'I'm really not looking forward to it.'

Mrs. Wright pulled up a chair and sat next to the young girl. 'Do you want to tell me about it?' she said. 'Why don't you want Christmas? It's the best time of the year.'

'I don't want my mum to go away.' Hannah's voice quivered and the single tear ran down her cheek. 'She's going to have a new baby. She's not been well and the doctor says she's got to go into hospital tomorrow. She won't be home for Christmas. She won't be home until the stupid new baby's been born.'

'I see,' said Mrs. Wright, slowly. 'I knew you were going to have a new baby brother or sister but I thought you'd be happy about it.'

'Well I was happy about it,' explained Hannah, 'but I don't want my mum to be in hospital for Christmas.'

'Listen,' said Mrs. Wright, 'when we start school again in January, you come and tell me all about your new baby brother or sister. Will you do that?'

'Yes I will,' sobbed Hannah, 'but I don't know if I am going to like our new baby.'

School restarted after the Christmas holiday on the 5th January. It was a cold, frosty morning, the type of morning when you could see your own breath, it was that cold. As soon as the children arrived in class, Hannah approached Mrs. Wright. She had a big smile on her face and a packet of photographs in her hand.

Mrs. Wright had not forgotten.

80

'Have you got some good news, Hannah?' she said, reaching for the photographs. 'Was everything O.K.?'

'I've got a new baby brother,' said Hannah, excitedly, 'and he was born on Christmas day, just like baby Jesus.'

'That's brilliant,' said Mrs. Wright. She took the photographs from the envelope and looked at each one with interest. 'He looks absolutely lovely, Hannah. So Christmas wasn't so bad after all, was it?'

'No, it was really good,' said Hannah. 'I went in to the hospital to visit on Christmas afternoon. There were decorations and there were carols playing and it was lovely. I'm really glad my brother was born on Christmas Day.'

'And tell me, as he was born on Christmas Day, has he got a special name?'

'Yes, he has,' said Hannah, looking surprised. 'How did you know he'd have a special name?'

Mrs. Wright looked pleased with herself. 'I bet he's called Christopher, or Nicholas after St. Nicholas,' she said, handing back the photographs.

Hannah looked disappointed. 'No,' she said, 'neither of those names. He's called Ryan after Ryan Giggs. My dad's a Manchester United supporter, you see, so he thought he'd choose a special name.'

'Lovely,' said Mrs. Wright, 'a lovely name - especially for someone born on Christmas day!'

Prayer: Dear Lord, we thank you for our families and for all who love and care for us at Christmas and throughout the year. Help us to appreciate the joy of giving, secure in the knowledge that you gave the world our saviour, Jesus Christ. Amen.

Follow up: Discuss the ways in which lives change when a new baby comes into the family. What sort of things change? Ask the children who has a young baby at home and what they do to help. Ask the children to say how they felt when their younger brother or sister was born. What was so important about the baby that was born over 2000 years ago? How did that special baby change the world?

THE STORM

Theme: The power of nature

Introduction: Obviously, this assembly is best used following a fierce storm. Talk to the children about how the storm built. What were the first signs that a storm was about to break? What does it mean when people refer to 'the calm before the storm'? Ask the children how they felt when the storm was raging. Can they give you words to describe the storm? You may wish to write the words on a white board or flip chart. Talk about what it must be like being out in the open during a storm.

The storm had been threatening all afternoon. Miss Dixon had warned the children that a storm was on the way but Peter had not taken much notice. True, it was really hot in school and the air felt heavy but, as Peter and his younger sister Helen made their way home, the sun was still trying to break through the gathering cloud. Not for long. By the time the children had reached home the sun had disappeared completely and the sky was darkening. Threatening black clouds were massing, gathering like a great army waiting to attack.

'There's a storm on the way,' said mum, staring out of the living room window. 'No doubt about it. It's ages since we had a real storm.'

'Everywhere's still and quiet,' said Helen, joining mum at the window. 'It doesn't feel like there's a storm on the way.'

'Calm before the storm,' said mum. 'I remember it well. I remember it from when I was a little girl. We used to have some terrible storms where I lived in Cornwall. Wrecker's storms, my grandfather used to call them.'

'I think I heard some thunder,' announced Peter, and they remained silent and listened. Sure enough there was a rumble in the distance as the sky turned even darker.

'It's not far away,' warned mum. 'It's a good job we're safe indoors. We must make sure Dexter doesn't get out.'

Dexter was the family dog and he was sitting in the middle of the room thumping his tail on the floor. He wondered what all the fuss was about.

The first flash of lightning came a few moments later and the thunder rumbled louder and nearer. The sky was almost black. It was as if time had become confused and night had arrived too early. And then the rain started. Slowly at first. A few huge drops falling from the sky and splattering on the dry ground. It soon gathered pace until it was a steady downpour and then an absolute deluge. There was a huge clap of thunder and a streak of lightning lit the blackened sky almost simultaneously. Helen jumped in shock and grabbed hold of her mum's arm. Dexter the dog dashed under the table and began to whine in fright.

'I don't know what all the fuss is about,' said Peter, casually. 'Nothing to be scared about.'

The next minute there was a tremendous explosion of thunder almost directly overhead and the sky seemed alive with lightening. It was so violent that the whole house shook.

Peter grabbed his mum's arm instinctively, the smile having completely disappeared from his face. Dexter ran upstairs and disappeared beneath the bed. The storm raged on, clap after clap of thunder and spectacular streaks of silver lightning. The rain was so heavy that it was impossible to see further than the front garden, which was awash with water, swirling across the sloped lawn like a fast flowing river.

The storm seemed to lodge overhead and it raged for forty minutes like an angry giant. And then the rain seemed to ease almost as quickly as it had started. The thunder and lightning grew more distant and the sky began to lighten as the storm passed on to vent its anger elsewhere.

'That was brilliant!' enthused Peter, releasing his hold on mum's arm. 'The best storm I've ever seen!'

'You didn't like it a few minutes ago,' said Helen accusingly. 'You were as scared as I was!'

'Rubbish!' said Peter. 'I was just making sure mum was all right!'

There was a pitiful whine from the stairs and Dexter appeared with his tail firmly between his legs and a face that looked as sad as a funeral.

'Poor Dexter,' said mum, walking across and picking him up. 'He doesn't understand what it's all about. Still, I don't think we'll see another storm like that for some time to come!'

Prayer: Help us to appreciate, Lord, the wonder and the power of Nature. Stormy weather can be spectacular and awesome but it can also be dangerous and frightening. When faced with such weather we ask that you protect those who are vulnerable and those without shelter. Teach us all to respect the wonderful world that you have made. Amen.

Follow up: The children may like to do their own research about storms. What causes thunder and lightning? Which parts of the world are more likely to face regular violent storms and why? The children could also use the library or Internet to research hurricanes and tornadoes.

'The Storm' is an excellent title for poetry. Begin with a brainstorming session to collect descriptive words and phrases, talk about the sequence of events leading up to and during a storm and then ask the children to write their own poems. Can some of the poems be presented at a subsequent assembly?

IT'S PANCAKE DAY!

Theme: Shrove Tuesday

Introduction: Begin by asking the children what special day it is today. Someone is sure to tell you that it is 'Pancake Day'. See if anyone can tell you that it is Shrove Tuesday and, if not, inform the children that Pancake Day is also known as Shrove Tuesday. You may wish to give the following factual information before reading the story:

Shrove Tuesday is the last day before the period which Christians call Lent - the forty days leading up to Easter. During Lent, Christians remember the time Jesus spent fasting in the wilderness. In the old days, the priest would 'shrove' his parishioners - meaning that he heard their confessions so that they could enter the fasting season with a clear conscience. People were not allowed to have milk, eggs or fat during Lent and, to use up all their supplies, they made pancakes.

Mrs. Matthews had arranged all the children around the small cooker, which had been placed at the front of the classroom. Next to the cooker was a table and on the table were a number of interesting ingredients. Year 2 were going to make pancakes!

'Now then,' said the teacher, which was how she always began her lessons, 'what do you think is the first thing we should do if we are going to make pancakes?'

Several hands shot up into the air and Mrs. Matthews pointed to an eager looking boy on the front row.

'Yes, Wesley, what do you think?'

'Turn the cooker on,' said Wesley, and he looked very pleased with himself.

'The cooker is already on,' said Mrs. Matthews, realising that she shouldn't have asked him in the first place. 'Has anyone else got an answer? Yes, Lisa?'

'We've got to make the batter,' answered Lisa, and Wesley frowned at her.

'Excellent,' said Mrs. Matthews. 'We've got to make the batter and that's what we're going to do now. Let's have a look at the ingredients, should we?'

Mrs. Matthews stood behind the small table and held each item up in turn.

'We've got eggs, some milk, plain flour, a pinch of salt and some butter to heat in the pan. That is all we need to make pancakes. And then I've got some sugar and lemon juice to put on the pancakes after we've made them.'

'Lovely!' said Wesley, licking his lips. 'Can I have the first one, Miss?'

'There'll be a taste for everyone, Wesley - but let's make them first, should we?'

The children watched as Mrs. Matthews began to mix the batter. She put the flour into a large bowl and made a hole in the centre. She broke an egg into the flour and then chose one of the children to break the next egg. She added half the milk and then stirred it with a wooden spoon before adding the remainder of the liquid.

'Come on, Wesley,' said Mrs. Matthews, when the mixture was almost ready. 'You can have a stir. You're good at stirring things!'
'Ugh! It looks like sloppy, yellow mud,' said Wesley as he swished the spoon round and round the bowl.

Mrs. Matthews heated the butter in the frying pan and moved the children a little further back before she poured in just enough batter to cover the bottom of the pan.

'We don't want them too thick,' she explained, as the mixture sizzled in the pan. 'We want them nice and light so that we can roll them up!'

Once the mixture started to set in the pan

Mrs. Matthews turned the pancake so that it would cook evenly on both sides.

'I know a rhyme about pancakes,' said the teacher.
>   'It goes like this:
>   Beat the batter in the bowl.
>   Heat the butter in the pan.
>   Toss the pancake if you can.'

'Are you going to toss the pancake?' asked Wesley. 'My mum tried to toss a pancake last year and it stuck to the kitchen ceiling. She was just looking up to see where it had gone when it landed on her head!'

'Thank you,' Wesley, said Mrs. Matthews. 'I'll have a go, should I?' And the teacher flipped the pancake into the air and caught it perfectly in the pan. The children clapped and let out a cheer.

Mrs. Matthews made several more pancakes until all the mixture was used up. And then came the best bit. She sprinkled them lightly with sugar, squirted them with lemon juice and cut them into pieces for the children to try. They were delicious.

'Lovely!' said Wesley, as the sugar and lemon juice dribbled down his chin. 'The best pancakes I've ever had, Mrs. Matthews.'

'Well, thank you,' said the teacher. 'Now then, once your hands are washed, we'll copy down the recipe and write about how we made them, should we?'

'If we have to,' said Wesley. 'I'd rather have another pancake, really.'

Prayer: Today is Shrove Tuesday. As we enjoy our pancakes, may we remember the time Jesus spent fasting in the wilderness and may we never forget what he gave up for us. As we enter Lent and move towards Easter, help us to make an extra effort to be kind, considerate and thoughtful people. Amen.

Follow up: An obvious follow up is for one or more of the classes to make their own pancakes.

The assembly can also be used as an introduction to Lent. Explain that Shrove Tuesday is the day before Ash Wednesday, which occurs forty days before Easter. You may wish to set the children a research task to find out why 'Ash Wednesday' is so called. In the USA, the last day before Lent is known as Mardi Gras, which is French for Fat Tuesday! It is a big occasion in New Orleans, Louisiana, where huge, colourful parades take place. Shrove Tuesday is often celebrated in Great Britain with traditional Pancake Races. Tell the children to watch the news as there is often an item about a Pancake Race.

NEVER TRUST A CROCODILE

Theme: Being aware of danger/Using common sense

Introduction: Unfortunately, it is a fact of life that you have always got to be aware of danger. Ask the children what dangers they may encounter as they live their daily lives. Talk about Road Safety, the need to be aware of Strangers, dangerous places to play. Explain that by using common sense together with previous knowledge it is almost always possible to avoid danger.

The following story illustrates that sometimes it is important to say 'no' when you are tempted to do something you know to be dangerous.

Two mischievous monkeys were playing together in the jungle. It was one of the hottest days of the year and Mo and Mal had been swinging around in the trees playing 'tig' for hours.

'I've had enough,' gasped Mal, sitting down beneath the shade of a great tree. 'I need a rest. I'm worn out.'

'I don't know about a rest,' said Mo, jumping down and joining his friend, 'I need a drink. Let's go down to the lake. The water's cool and refreshing. We can have a drink and we can go for a swim to cool off.'

'But my mum said I wasn't to go near the lake,' said Mal, looking concerned. 'My mum said Mr. Crocodile lives in the lake and he likes nothing better for his dinner than a nice young monkey. That's what my mum said.'

'Nonsense,' said Mo. 'I've been for a swim in the lake lots of times and I've never yet seen Mr. Crocodile. Are you coming with me, or what?'

'All right,' agreed Mal, reluctantly, 'but if there's any sign of that nasty crocodile, I'm off. I'm going home.'

Five minutes later the two monkeys left the safety of the trees and stood on the shore of the great lake. The clear water sparkled in the midday sunshine. It looked cool, inviting and crocodile free.

'What did I tell you,' said Mo, dipping his foot in the clear, refreshing water. 'No sign of any danger.'

Mal was just about to join his friend when he noticed two green eyes staring at him. They seemed to be floating on the surface of the lake, just a couple of metres from the shoreline. Mal let out a shriek and leapt back from the water's edge.

'What's the matter?' said Mo, as he waded further into the water. 'Have you been bitten by a mosquito?'

Mal pointed into the water and said, 'L-l-look! There in the water! It's that nasty, dangerous crocodile!'

As the two monkeys looked on, a great, green, wrinkled head poked out of the water and there was Mr. Crocodile, a smile on his face, a glint in his eye.

'Good day to you,' said Mr. Crocodile, and he waded a little closer. 'I can see you are very observant but did I hear you call me dangerous?' He took another couple of steps towards the monkeys.

'Surely you can see that I'm not dangerous? I'm a very friendly crocodile. I'm just having a rest in the cool water.'

'Move back!' shouted Mal to his friend. 'Come out of the water!'

'A rest in the cool water,' repeated Mo, making no effort to return to shore. 'Yes, it is a very hot and tiring day, isn't it?'

'Very tiring,' agreed Mr. Crocodile, and he opened his mouth in a wide yawn, displaying two rows of razor sharp teeth.

'Look at his teeth!' shouted Mal, and he leapt up and down on the shoreline.

'Come out of the water, Mo!'

'We've been playing tig,' explained Mo, as Mr. Crocodile moved ever closer. 'We've come down to the lake to cool off.'

'Good idea,' said the crocodile. He was so close that Mo could see the whites of his eyes. 'I've got a favourite game of my own?'

'What's that?' enquired Mo, innocently. 'What game do you like to play?'

'SNAP!' said the crocodile, and his great mouth opened and closed so quickly that Mal didn't even see his friend disappear.

Prayer: We know, Lord, that as we live our daily lives we face many dangers. Give us the knowledge and the common sense to keep ourselves safe. May we never be tempted to do anything that could harm others or ourselves. Amen.

Follow up: The children could write a short story to illustrate the theme DANGER. Begin by brainstorming some of the dangers they should be aware of: e.g. busy roads, railway lines, strangers, building sites etc. Alternatively, the children could write a poem entitled 'Don't'. To warn others about dangers.

Discuss the problem of 'temptation'. It is easy to follow others when you are part of a group, even if you know that you are doing wrong. It takes a great deal of strength and courage to say 'No'.

THINK WHAT YOU ARE DOING

Theme: The importance of concentration

Introduction: Play a quick game of concentration. Have a tray ready with a selection of common items - a ruler, pencil, rubber, stapler etc. Bring a child out to look at the items, make the child turn away and remove one item. Can the child tell you which item is missing? Repeat this a couple of times. Explain to the children that the game was just a bit of fun. However, it is important to concentrate, especially at school. Good concentration means that you learn more and learning to concentrate prepares you for life.

The problem with Harry was that he never really concentrated on what he was doing. He never really tried his best. He distracted other children in his class and he was easily distracted himself. For example, he was forever talking instead of concentrating on his work. It was not that he couldn't do his work, it was more that he couldn't be bothered to do his work. His teacher, Mrs. Willis, had already moved him three times and she felt sorry for anyone sitting next to Harry, he was such a chatterbox.

'It's no wonder you never get your work finished,' she said to him, one Monday morning. 'You can't concentrate for more than two minutes at a time! I want you to make a real effort this week so that I can give your mum and dad a better report when I see them on Parents' Evening.'

Harry did not have a good week. He was already in trouble by Monday afternoon. Instead of concentrating on his artwork he had leaned across the table and spilt the water container. There was dirty water everywhere. It ruined all the pictures and six children had to start again. Harry was sent to sit on his own.

On Tuesday morning, Harry's hand-writing was a disgrace. He found it boring copying down the same words over and over again and so he wrote as quickly as he could so that he had some spare time. Mrs. Willis hit the roof.

'What on earth is that,' she said, jabbing a finger towards Harry's untidy scrawl. 'It looks as if it has been done by an alien! You will stay in on your own this playtime and do it all again!'

Wednesday went reasonably well until the football match. Harry had only played a few games for the school team. Mr. Hughes had told him that he was a good footballer but that he had to learn to concentrate on his own position and not interfere with other people's jobs. However, two children were off school ill and so Harry was drafted into the team. It was an important cup match and Harry was asked to play in defence on the right side of the pitch. As soon as the whistle blew he was all over the place - on the left, in the middle, he even went up to take a corner. Mr. Hughes was hopping mad on the touchline but Harry took no notice. By half time his team were two nil down and by full time they had lost by five goals to nil. Even Harry realised that four of the goals could have been prevented if he had been in position.

Harry was a little more subdued on Thursday. He was not popular with the other boys, who blamed him for losing the football match.

He still managed to drop his dinner tray on the floor at lunchtime. He had been turning round and talking while carrying his tray and he walked straight into a table.

Thursday Evening was Parents' Evening and Mrs. Willis had made up her mind to tell Harry's mum and dad exactly what he was like. They were not surprised when they heard the report; in fact, they were just as frustrated as the teacher was.

'Of course, we'll talk to him,' said Harry's mum, 'but he's just as bad at home. He can't even sit and watch television without fidgeting. He drives us mad!'

'I'll have another talk to him,' said Mrs. Willis. 'I have to tell you that unless he improves his concentration he is going to fall behind in his work - and it will be a real struggle to catch up!'

So Mrs. Willis did talk to Harry, on the Friday of that very same week. She kept him behind after school until the room was quiet and empty of other children so that Harry could concentrate on what she had to say. She looked serious and Harry was ready to listen.

It had been a bad week.

'You know you can't go on like this, Harry,' began Mrs. Willis. 'You really have got to make more effort to concentrate. What do you want to be when you grow up Harry?'

'I don't know,' said Harry, looking puzzled. 'I haven't thought.'

'A doctor?' suggested Mrs. Willis. 'A racing driver? A road sweeper? It doesn't really matter what you want to be, does it Harry? Whatever you do in life you have got to concentrate. Just imagine if you are a surgeon performing a delicate operation and you lose your concentration; or you are a racing driver travelling at terrific speed on a difficult circuit; or even if you are a road sweeper on a busy main road with great lorries thundering past. Just think what might happen if you lose your concentration.'

For once, Harry was listening, looking directly at the teacher, concentrating on what she had to say.

'You will get nowhere in life unless you learn to concentrate, Harry. You will fall further and further behind and you'll become more and more unhappy.'

The teacher stared at him for a moment and then continued. 'Why don't you make up your mind to try harder, Harry? Why don't you make a real effort next week? Really concentrate and show us all what you are capable of achieving. What do you think?'

'I think it's a good idea,' replied Harry, and for the first time in his life - he really meant what he said.

Prayer: Dear Lord, may we always try to do our best in everything we do. Help us to concentrate at all times so that we increase our knowledge and skills in preparation for life and so that we keep others and ourselves safe. Amen.

Follow up: Tell the children you are going to ask them a few questions to see who was concentrating on the story. Ask what disaster happened because of Harry's lack of concentration on Monday. Why did he get into trouble on Tuesday? What position was he asked to play in the football match? What was the final score in the match? What happened on Thursday lunchtime?

Mrs. Willis mentioned three possible jobs when she was talking to Harry. Why is it important to concentrate in all three jobs?

Ask the children for other examples of how lack of concentration could lead to danger. The examples could be around school, at home or out on the streets.

THE JOURNEY

Theme: Our wonderful universe/space exploration

Introduction: Ask the children if they have a favourite holiday place that they like to visit. Select a couple of children to explain why they like their chosen place. Ask for a show of hands to see how many children have been on an aeroplane. What is good/bad about flying? Explain how amazing it is that you can travel to the other side of our planet in a matter of hours. Our ancestors would have thought that impossible. Human beings will always strive to reach new boundaries and usually they are successful.

Tell the children to listen carefully to the story - not everything is as it seems. Explain that you are going to ask them a question half way through the story.

Mr. and Mrs. Powell, Philip and Laura unfastened their seat belts and settled down for the long flight. Take off had been very smooth, although Laura did complain that they'd gone that fast her ears had popped! The Powell family had been looking forward to this trip for months. Of course, they had been on holidays together before but this was something different, altogether more exciting. Nobody else from school was travelling to the same destination and Philip's teacher had made him promise to take lots of photographs and video clips with his digital camera to show everyone when he got back.

Mrs. Powell had felt a little nervous about the flight but now, as she sat back in her comfortable, spacious seat, she felt excited as she thought about what lay ahead of them.

They had been travelling for about an hour when the first of their meals arrived. This was just what Laura had been waiting for! She was starving!

'Chicken with roast potatoes and vegetables,' announced the stewardess, handing out the pre-packed containers. 'Followed by fresh fruit salad and washed down with tea, coffee or fruit juice.'

'This is great,' said Laura, peeling back the foil lid. 'Can I have yours, Philip?'

'No you can't!' snapped her brother. 'Don't be so greedy!'

The family finished their meals and, feeling full and content, they settled down to enjoy their journey.

Stop reading at this point and ask the children if they can guess where the family are going for their holiday. Continue reading after a few answers have been given.

Philip had a window seat and the view was spectacular. Planet Earth had been left far behind. It had been fabulous watching it fade into the distance; the blue planet teeming with life, home to millions and millions of humans, plants and animals. The craft was travelling through space at terrific speed, yet the journey was so smooth. There was no turbulence as there had been when Philip had flown by aeroplane. Space was fantastic, dark in one sense but lit by thousands of distant, shining stars. Of course, Philip and Laura all about space from their computer stations at school. In addition, they had both been on a simulated flight but this was totally different; this was the real thing.

Philip began to wonder what the space station would be like. He had seen video footage and he and Laura had visited it through the Virtual Reality facility on his computer but it was exciting to think that in less than twenty four hours time they would be there, inside the great dome, walking on the surface of another planet. Philip thought back to his history lessons at school. It was funny to think that only seventy five years ago Man first set foot on the moon. Space exploration had come a long way since 1969 when Neil Armstong had stepped out of the lunar module onto the Sea of Tranquillity. Here they were, on their way to a distant planet.

Philip looked round to see that his sister was already asleep. That seemed a good idea. It was going to be a long and tiring flight. He put his head back against the seat rest and closed his eyes and, in less than a minute he was drifting away, dreaming of the fantastic adventure that lay before him.

Prayer: We thank you, Lord, for the wonders of the universe. We look up into the night sky and cannot begin to imagine its infinity. We thank you for the stars and the planets and for Man's achievements in space exploration. We do not know what the future holds but we ask that everything we do may be for the benefit of mankind. Amen.

Follow up: Firstly, set a challenge. See who is the first child to give the correct year in which the story is set. (It can be worked out adding on seventy five years from the first moon landing).

The story provides a starting point for work about space and space exploration. Children can research about the solar system or about a particular planet. Further research could cover the first manned space flight and the first moon landing.

Points for discussion may include the following:
  How likely is it that families will holiday in space in the future?
  Will it be possible to set up a space station on another planet?
  Is it likely that we will find other life in outer space?
  What will schools be like in the future? Will there be teachers or will all learning be done from computer stations?

MAC THE MONKEY'S HELPFUL DAY

Theme: Helping others

Introduction: Explain to the pupils how you like children to be kind and helpful at all times. Ask children to nominate someone from their own class who has been helpful recently and discuss their responses. Have there been any examples of children being helpful without having to be asked? See if the children can give examples of ways in which they have been helpful at home. You may like to mention someone who has been helpful to you recently - a child, another member of staff, a parent etc.

Mac the Monkey was bored. He just did not know what to do with himself. He paced up and down at the bottom of the tree house, tutting and sighing loudly, doing his best to attract mum's attention.

'Whatever is the matter with you, Mac?' said Mrs. Monkey, breaking from her housework and staring hard at her son.

'Why don't you give me a hand tidying up - make yourself useful if you've got nothing better to do?'

'I'm bored,' explained Mac, putting his monkey hands on his hips, 'and I hate tidying up. You know I do.'

'Yes, but it would be nice to get a little help from time to time,' said mum. 'After all, you've nothing better to do, have you?'

'I think I'll go for a walk,' said Mac, making his mind up quickly. 'Yes, I'll go for a nice, restful walk in the jungle.'

And Mrs. Monkey sighed and carried on with the housework as Mac disappeared into the nearby trees.

Mac really didn't like helping around the house and every time the word 'help' was mentioned, he made an excuse to do something else.

'I'll help when I'm older,' he muttered to himself, as he kicked the leaves beneath his feet. 'Yes, that's what I'll do, I'll help when I'm older.'

Mac was whistling to himself as he walked along. It was a beautiful day and he hadn't a care in the world. He had not gone far when he stopped, suddenly, and twitched his monkey ears. Surely that was a cry for help he could hear.

'Help! Help!' The voice was high pitched and desperate.

Mac pushed his way through some dense bushes and found himself facing a fast flowing stream, the waters swelled by recent heavy rain. A squirrel was trapped in the middle of the stream, stranded on a small muddy island, the fast flowing water racing past on either side of him.

'Help!' Yelled the squirrel. 'I was crossing the stream when the bank burst and now I'm stuck. Help.'

Mac looked around, quickly. Yes, there was a tree near the edge of the stream with a long vine dangling into the clear water. Mac grabbed the end of the vine and climbed the tree.

'Are you ready?' He shouted to the squirrel, and then he launched himself into the air. 'Tar - zan!' he shouted as he swung across the stream, and when he reached the middle he grabbed hold of the squirrel's bushy tail and sailed across with him to the bank opposite.

'Oh, thank you so much,' said the shaken squirrel. 'I wish everyone was as helpful as you.'

'Yes, I suppose I am,' said Mac, proudly, and he continued on his way.

A little further along the track Mac heard a very strange noise. It was as if there was a rumbling sound coming from beneath the ground. Mac moved carefully towards the sound - and nearly fell head first into a deep pit. He just recovered in time and stood balanced dangerously on the edge.

'Help me!' came a deep voice from down below. 'Please help me before the hunters come back!'

Mac stared into the pit and saw two frightened eyes staring back at him. It was Mr. Lion, trapped by the humans who would soon return to see what they had caught.

'It's all right,' shouted Mac. 'I'll soon get you out. Don't go away!' And he turned and looked all around in desperation.

Then it came to him. Branches! He needed lots of branches to throw into the pit so that Mr. Lion could climb out. Mac scrambled off into the trees and bushes, pulling wildly at any loose branches he could find. Within minutes he had thrown enough into the hunter's pit for Mr. Lion to make a platform. As Mac looked on, Mr. Lion leapt out of the pit and landed within centimetres of the startled monkey. Mr. Lion shook his great mane and roared at the top of his voice.

'Thank you, Mac,' he said, and Mac was sure he saw a tear trickle from Mr. Lion's eye. 'You saved my life. You're the most helpful monkey I've ever met!'

'The most helpful monkey he's ever met,' repeated Mac, as he made his way home.

He felt so proud of himself. If only he had known earlier that helping others could be so satisfying. 'Wait until I tell mum that I'm the most helpful monkey he's ever met!' And then a twinge of guilt pricked his conscience. After all, he wasn't very helpful at home. He had refused to help his mum that very morning.

Mac made up his mind there and then. He would not say anything about Mr. Lion or about the trapped squirrel. No, he would keep that secret - but he would start helping at home. He really was determined to be the most helpful monkey in the jungle.

Prayer: Please Lord, help us grow up to be kind and considerate people who will always do others a good turn. May selfish thoughts never rise to the surface. Help us to be pleasant and cheerful as we go about our daily lives. Amen.

Follow up: Ask how many children help their parents regularly at home. What sort of jobs do they do? How many children complain when they are asked to tidy up their room? Why do parents ask for help?

Tell the children that you are going to look for examples of pupils being helpful around school. Bring such examples to their attention at a subsequent assembly.

THE PEOPLE NEXT DOOR

Theme: Good Neighbours/Learning to judge people by what they are and not how they look

Introduction: Begin by asking the children who has good next door neighbours. Choose a couple of children and ask why they think they have good neighbours. What is it that makes a good neighbour? Look for words such as 'friendly,' 'kind,' 'considerate.' Discuss the fact that there are often stories in the newspapers and even programmes on television about awful neighbours who often feud with each other over all sorts of things. Give any examples that you are able to find. How much more pleasant it is to live next door to people you get on with. Tell them to listen carefully to the story that follows, as there are a few points for discussion.

We didn't get on with the people next door. My dad just referred to them as 'the Hobsons'. There were five of them, altogether - Mr. and Mrs. Hobson, Tracy Hobson and her younger brother, Jason and their awful dog, who for some reason they called Butch. I can't think of a less suitable name for a dog. It would have been better called Matchstick it was that thin and scrawny.

It wasn't that we were snobs or anything like that - but if you'd met the Hobson's you'd be glad they didn't live next door to you. The way they looked, for a start. They never seemed to have any new clothes. They wore the same things day in day out, summer or winter. Tracy Hobson was in the same class as me at school and I can remember her wearing the same blue anorak for about two years. It got far too small for her and her arms used to stick out of the sleeves like flagpoles. Then one day she came in something different and when I looked, there was her brother Jason wearing Tracy's familiar blue anorak. I didn't appreciate at that time that the Hobson's didn't have much money. I didn't understand that Mr. Hobson had suffered an accident at the factory and was unable to work.

And then there was the noise. Mrs. Hobson had the radio on from the minute she got up in the morning. To make matters worse, Mr. Hobson would put the television on at the same time. It used to drive my parents mad. My dad said something once and it got better for a while - but it didn't last. The dog was as bad. They used to turn it out into the back yard first thing in the morning and it would bark none stop for hours, until it got a sore throat and couldn't bark any more. It really was hard work living next door to the Hobson's.

But let me tell you about the night we were burgled. It was December, leading up to Christmas, and we had gone to see my auntie and uncle who lived a couple of miles away. We'd gone to deliver their presents, as we always did just before Christmas. Dad had been careful to lock the house. He was very fussy about security. It came as a shock to us, therefore, when we arrived home at about half past nine to find a police car outside our front door, blue light flashing into the night. There was a policeman standing by our gate and he had his hand on Mr. Hobson's shoulder. Mrs. Hobson was in the background with Tracy and Jason and Butch was doing his best to bark, considering the time of night.

96

We could see at once that our front door was open and we all immediately realised what had happened.

'I don't believe it,' said dad. 'That man's got some explaining to do?'

Dad got out of the car and slammed the door shut behind him. We all followed him out onto the pavement.

Before any of us could speak, the policeman looked at dad and said, 'Is this your property, Sir?'

'It certainly is,' replied dad, and he gave Mr. Hobson an icy stare.

'Well you've been very lucky,' continued the policeman. 'It's a good job you've got such good neighbours. 'If it wasn't for Mr. Hobson and Butch the thief would have got away with most of your Christmas shopping,' and he patted Mr. Hobson on the shoulder and indicated towards the police car.

We looked over to see another policeman sitting inside the car with a scruffy looking youth. The youth was clutching his arm where Butch had bitten him.

My dad's mouth dropped open in astonishment. 'I don't know what to say,' he stammered.

'Well, you could try saying thank you,' said the policeman. 'It's always a good start, you know.'

And my dad reached forward and shook Mr. Hobson warmly by the hand.

It's funny, but we looked upon the Hobson's very differently from that day on. It's great to have such good neighbours living next door to you - don't you agree?

Prayer: Help us, Lord, to be good neighbours at all times. Teach us not to judge people by how they look but to accept people for what they are. May we grow up to be tolerant people who appreciate the many differences that go to make up our wonderful world. Amen.

Follow up: There are several points for discussion. How did the family feel about the Hobson's in the early part of the story? What was it about the Hobson's that the family did not like? What did the family think had happened when they returned home to find their house had been burgled? Why do you think they jumped to the conclusion that the Hobson's were responsible?

Reinforce the message that you cannot judge people solely by the way they look.

A challenging task would be for the children to write a story in which some apparently good neighbours are not what they seem.

HAVE A LITTLE PATIENCE

Theme: Patience

Introduction: Tell the children that 'patience is a virtue' and ask what they think is the meaning of the sentence. What is a virtue? Can the children think of any other virtues? e.g. honesty, truthfulness etc. Ask the children if they have ever had to be patient for anything? Sometimes if you have to be patient and wait for something good it is all the more enjoyable.

Connor had a lot of good qualities but patience was not one of them. He was an intelligent boy who was capable of doing really well at school but, because he was so impatient, he often rushed through tasks and made careless mistakes. His teacher, Mrs. Hughes, found him very frustrating.

'Slow down, Connor,' she would say. 'You're always in a rush. It's not a race to finish. Patience is always rewarded.'

Connor was the same at home. He drove his mother mad - so much so that his father would lose patience with him and end up shouting. They were both as bad as each other.

One Saturday afternoon, as a treat, Connor's mum said she would pay for the family to go to the cinema. There was a new adventure film out about dinosaurs that Connor really wanted to see. However, when they arrived at the cinema, the queue was so long it stretched half way around the building.

'That's ridiculous,' said Connor, waving an arm in the general direction of the queue. 'What's the point of standing at the back of that long line? We'll never get in!'

'Of course we will,' said Sophie, Connor's younger sister. 'You've just got to wait your turn and be patient.'

'Well, I don't fancy waiting with that lot,' said dad. 'You can wait if you want. Connor and I will go to watch the football game. Rovers are at home this afternoon and it should be a good match. We'll catch up with you later.'

Mum and Sophie shrugged their shoulders and joined the queue.

Half an hour later Connor and his father arrived at the football ground. It had begun to rain steadily and, to their horror, there were queues everywhere.

'I don't believe it,' said Connor, in frustration. 'Queues should be banned. What a waste of time.'

'Come on,' said dad, 'there's a turnstile on the other side of the ground where there's never a queue.'

Dad was right. He and Connor paid their money and walked straight into the stadium. There was a problem however. They had paid to sit in the only part of the ground that was uncovered and the rain was getting heavier and heavier.

By half time Connor and his dad were soaked and Rovers were 2-0 down. Dad bought Connor a pie and a hot cup of tea to cheer him up but Connor was in such a hurry to

98

drink it he spilt it down the front of his jacket. The tea burned him and as he jumped up, he dropped his pie and stood on it.

The second half was no better. Rovers did everything but score. They hit the bar, they hit the post and they missed an open goal. The rain fell persistently.

With five minutes to go Connor said, 'I've had enough. Can we go home dad?'

'Good idea,' said dad. 'We'll get out before the crowd. I haven't the patience to fight my way through this lot.'

They heard the first cheer just as they left the stadium.

'I don't believe it!' said Connor. 'The moment we walk out, Rovers score!'

The second huge cheer came moments later. Connor and his dad just stared at each other in disbelief. They were completely speechless.

When they arrived home half an hour later, dripping wet and totally depressed, Sophie came running up to them.

'The film was brilliant,' she said, 'the best I've ever seen. You really should have waited. Still, at least you saw Rovers get a good draw, eh? The last five minutes must have been really exciting!'

'Sort of,' muttered Connor, his face bright red. He just hadn't the patience to explain.

Prayer: We ask, Lord, that you give us the patience to deal sensibly with the many problems in life. It seems that we are often in too much of a hurry to do anything properly. Make us stop and think before we rush into things and make mistakes. Guard us and guide us in your way. Amen.

Follow up: Ask the children to think back to the story. What examples of impatience can they remember? What happened as a result of impatience?

Can the children think of any other examples where patience is required to complete a task well? (e.g. learning to play a musical instrument, learning a special dance or gymnastic routine, practising ball skills etc.)

YOU ARE WHAT YOU EAT

Theme: Healthy Eating

> **Introduction:** Have some pictures ready of healthy and unhealthy foods. You can usually find examples in the Sunday magazines. Have a white board available at the front of assembly. On the white board, draw two sections marked 'healthy' and 'unhealthy'. Hold up each picture in turn and ask the children into which section they should be placed. You could choose a child from each class in turn. When all the pictures have been sorted, explain to the children that what they eat can effect their health and the way in which they live their lives.

Paula was always tired. It did not seem to matter what time she went to bed, she still woke up feeling tired. In the morning, Paula would often stay in bed until the last possible moment.

'I'm just getting out!' she would shout down to her mum, as she pulled the covers further over her head. 'I'm putting my socks on!'

When she finally tumbled out of bed, she would be so late that the rest of her routine had to be rushed. She often had a packet of crisps and a glass of cola for breakfast. She could drink the cola in three gulps and she could eat the crisps on her way to school. Her mother was not happy with the situation, but she had to get Paula's little brother ready for Nursery and, as Paula was ten years old, she had not got time to fuss over her. So Paula arrived at school each morning feeling tired and lethargic.

Paula did not really mix with the other children at playtimes. Her classmates played all sorts of games and they always asked Paula if she wanted to play - but it seemed too much trouble - too much like hard work. Paula preferred to stand to one side, against the wall, where she could eat her playtime snack in peace. She usually brought her favourite chewy toffee bar for her playtime snack. It was so sticky that it seemed to take her all playtime to eat it - so she couldn't join in the games - she hadn't time. Also, she'd been having a problem with toothache lately. She seemed to get a pain on the right side of her mouth every time she chewed, which in Paula's case was quite often. She would have to tell her mum so that she could arrange an appointment with the dentist. It would be fair to say that Paula was not very happy with her life.

One bright Monday afternoon Paula and her classmates returned to their room after lunch to find the teacher's desk covered with food and drink. There were tins and packets, fresh fruit and vegetables, bottles of milk, bottles of water and tins of cola. There were also chocolate bars and sweets, which made Paula's eyes light up.

Mrs. Philips, Paula's teacher, settled the children, took the register and then announced: 'Right, children. We're going to begin our new topic. We're going to be learning about healthy eating,' she smiled at the children. 'My mother used to have a saying. She used to say: You are what you eat. Do you know, children, there's a lot of truth in that.'

The children looked puzzled but they were all listening attentively.

'Let's look at the food before us and see if we can sort it into two categories - healthy and unhealthy. I'm going to hold each item up in turn and I want you to decide. Is it healthy or unhealthy?'

Mrs. Philips picked up a bunch of carrots and held them in the air. Paula hated carrots. Definitely unhealthy.

'Well, children?'

'Healthy, Miss,' said Emma Jones.

'Of course they are,' confirmed the teacher. 'So we'll put them on this side of the table and we'll talk about why they are healthy later on.'

Mrs. Philips picked up a bottle of water and waved it in the air. 'Unhealthy,' thought Paula. 'Absolutely tasteless.'

'Healthy,' said Jamie Jordan, and Mrs. Philips confirmed that his answer was correct.

She placed the water next to the carrots and picked up a packet of fruit gums.

'That's more like it,' thought Paula. 'I love fruit gums. They must be healthy because they make me feel happy.'

Of course, she was wrong. 'Very bad for you,' said Mrs. Philips. 'Full of additives, colouring and sugar. Too many of these and you'll end up with rotten teeth!'

Paula rubbed her jaw. She hadn't been to the dentist yet and she was still having problems.

As the lesson progressed, Paula became more and more interested. When the sorting was finished, she looked at the table in horror. All the things she liked, the things she ate and drank most, were on the unhealthy side. The other side was full of things she never ate - different types of fruit and vegetables, milk and water, yoghurt and cereals. Mrs. Philips went on to explain about protein and vitamins and how eating the wrong type of food could make you feel permanently tired and grumpy.

'I feel permanently tired and grumpy,' thought Paula, staring at the pile of unhealthy food.

'If you want to look better, feel fitter and have lots more energy,' said Mrs. Philips, 'then make sure you eat a sensible, healthy diet. It doesn't mean you can't have a little treat now and again - but remember what my mum said: You are what you eat. I think there are one or two children in this class who might need to change their habits a little bit.'

Paula smiled and nodded her head in agreement.

Prayer: We know, Lord, that we can do a great deal to keep ourselves healthy. Help us to look after ourselves and to live our lives in a sensible way. May we eat and drink the right things for a healthy body and may we follow your way for a healthy mind. Amen.

Follow up: More detailed follow up could concentrate on why different foods are good or bad for you. Why, for example, is a diet rich in fruit and vegetables healthy?
The children could have a look at the school meals menu for the week to see if it provides a balanced, healthy diet.

Classes could hold a survey of favourite foods/drinks/fruit etc. The results could be tabulated in a graph and shown in assembly.

Discuss what other action is required to ensure a high level of fitness and health. (Regular exercise, the correct amount of sleep etc.).

JENNA'S PATCH

Theme: Appreciation of plants/Awareness of the environment

Introduction: Start by asking the children if any of them have a favourite plant or flower. Alternatively, bring in a few seasonal flowers and see if the children can identify them. Ask if any of the children help their parents to look after the garden. Why do some houses have gardens? Explain that trees, shrubs, plants and flowers help to brighten up our lives. They are also very important to the environment as they provide oxygen. As people grow and learn more about plants, gardening often becomes a hobby that can last for a lifetime.

Jenna's mum and dad loved gardening and they tried to encourage Jenna whenever they could. As they wandered round the garden they would talk about the different types of plants and Jenna would try to learn the names. Jenna was only six years old and she struggled with some of the long names. She could manage pansy and dahlia but mesumbryanthemum was hard to say for a six year old, especially for a six year old with two front teeth missing.

One bright spring morning, as Jenna was walking around the garden with her mum, she suddenly announced:

'I'd like a patch of garden of my own.'

'Would you, now,' said mum, smiling. 'Well, we'll have to see what we can do, won't we?' Mum pointed towards an area in the right hand corner of the garden and said, 'What if we make your patch over here?'

Jenna looked at the area and pulled a face.

'It's all covered in grass,' she said. 'Nothing will grow there.'

'We'll have to clear it,' explained mum. 'Gardens don't just appear, you know. You have to work hard on them. We'll start on Saturday. We'll get dad to help.'

And they did. That same Saturday mum, dad and Jenna got to work clearing the patch of grass and weeds. It was hard work. Dad took off the top surface of grass, mum dug the ground and Jenna used the hoe to break up the soil ready for planting. It took them more than two hours but by the time they had finished there was a clear, rectangular patch of soil just waiting for a selection of plants.

'Right,' said Jenna, looking at her new patch, 'what shall we put into it.'

'That's up to you,' said dad. 'It's your patch, remember?'

'But I haven't got anything,' said Jenna. 'How can I make it nice if I haven't got anything to put in it?'

'I'll tell you what,' said mum, 'we'll take a trip to the Garden Centre, but you'll have to use some of your pocket money to buy some plants. All right?'

'That's fine,' said Jenna. 'I want to use my money because it's my patch!'

Forty-five minutes later, Jenna arrived at Prettywood Garden Centre with her mum and dad. It was quite crowded and Jenna didn't know where to begin.

'You need to decide what you want to grow in your patch,' explained dad, 'then we can find the right section in the garden centre.'

Jenna thought for a moment and then she said, 'I want to grow something to look at and something to eat!'
Dad laughed and said, 'Come on, I think I know where we can make a start.'

Dad took Jenna inside the shop to a section that sold seeds. He found the vegetable seeds and removed a packet from the shelf.

'There you are,' he said, passing the packet to Jenna. 'Runner beans. Nice and easy to grow, lovely red flowers and then delicious beans to eat later in summer. What do you think?'

'Yes,' said Jenna, looking at the picture on the packet. 'I want to grow them up a wigwam of canes like it shows on the packet.'

'Fine,' said dad, and he dropped the seeds into a basket and moved on to the flower section.

Jenna had a lovely time. She chose a packet of nasturtiums and a packet of sunflowers. Mum came in with a tray of pansies, some of the flowers already opening, brightly coloured like smiling faces. She could have chosen lots more but she didn't have enough pocket money.

'You've got plenty there,' said mum. 'You've only got to fill your patch, not the whole garden you know.'

When they arrived home, they went straight back out into the garden and started to plant the seeds. Mum made a wigwam of canes in the middle of the patch and Jenna pushed the seeds into the soil around the base of the canes. She planted the sunflowers towards the back of her patch. Mum explained that they grew very tall and they needed the fence for support. She scattered the nasturtiums around and planted the pansies along the front edge. When she had finished, she stood back and folded her arms in satisfaction.

'That's the easy bit,' said mum. 'Now you've got to look after your patch to make sure everything grows. You'll have to water it if it becomes too dry, tie the beans and the sunflowers up when they start to grow and check it regularly to make sure there aren't too many weeds. If you do all of that I think you'll have a really nice patch!'

'I'll look after it,' promised Jenna. 'I'll look after it. You just wait and see.'

Prayer: We thank you, Lord, for all living things. We think especially, this morning, of the variety of plants and trees that exist in our wonderful world. May we learn to appreciate the beauty and the value of plants and do all we can to cultivate and protect them. Amen.

Follow up: Does the school have a garden or an environmental area that can be tended by the children? If not, could an area be developed? If this is not possible is there a small area inside school that could be set aside for an indoor garden?

If the story is used in spring, the children could sow seeds and grow their own plants. You could choose some of the varieties mentioned in the story. Coleus are easy to grow and are ideal for young children as they produce beautiful foliage.

A collection of different plants provides a stimulating opportunity for an art lesson. Encourage the children to produce observational drawings or paintings. The finished work could be displayed together with the plants in a prominent area.

I'M TOO HOT

Theme: Hot summer weather

Introduction: There will not be many days in the year when you can use this assembly! Save it for a hot spell when it will be most relevant.

Ask the children how they feel when the weather is really hot and sunny. There will probably be a variety of responses. There can be no doubt that a lovely, sunny morning makes people feel happier and most children enjoy playing out in the sunshine. However, very hot weather can also make you tired and grumpy - especially if you have to work hard in school. Ask the children how they would describe their perfect day.

'I'm too hot,' complained Laura, as she sat at the breakfast table eating her Cornflakes and cold milk. 'I don't like being too hot.'

'Don't be silly,' said mum. 'It's a lovely morning. The sun is shining and there isn't a cloud in the sky. You'd be complaining more if it was raining.'

'But I don't like it too hot,' continued Laura. 'It makes me feel all grumpy.'

'I'd noticed,' said mum. 'I don't understand how anyone can be in a bad mood on such a lovely day.'

It was early July and the past week had been glorious. The sun had shone every day and the temperature seemed to be rising steadily. All the children at Laura's school were in their summer uniforms and many had taken in sun hats or baseball caps to protect themselves from the heat of the sun during break and lunchtime. Laura had been fine for the first few days but it was near the end of term, she was tired and the heat was making her irritable. She finished her breakfast and set off for school with her mum, bag in hand, hat on head.

'It's too far to walk,' she grumbled, as she dragged a few paces behind mum. 'I don't see why we can't use the car.'

'That would be really lazy,' explained mum. 'We only live three roads away from school.'

'My bag's too heavy,' said Laura, hitching it further onto her shoulder. 'I don't see why I have to bring all these books home.'

'Laura, stop complaining!' said mum. She was beginning to lose patience. 'You'll be on holiday next week. I bet you won't be complaining about the heat when you're playing on the beach.'

'That's different,' snapped Laura, and with one final grumble she said, 'and I look stupid in this sun hat. I look like a great big flower!'

To be fair, it was the hottest day of the year. The sun shone straight into Laura's classroom during the morning and, even though it was fitted with blinds, the room became stifling. After morning break, Mrs. Challendar, Laura's teacher, took the children outside and sat them in the shade. It was still hot, for there was little breeze, but it was more pleasant than being in the classroom.

Mrs. Challendar talked to the children about coping with the heatwave.

'You have to use a lot of common sense,' she explained. 'If you're in the sun for any length of time you should use protective cream. It's a good idea to wear a hat, as well. The one Laura uses is ideal.

Laura smiled and felt proud.

'Don't go chasing around or running about too much when it's so hot,' continued Mrs. Challendar. 'There are plenty of places around our school yard where you can find some shade and we're very lucky to have such big trees on the school field.'

'My mum says you should drink plenty of fresh water when it's hot,' said Jamie Clegg. 'It stops you from being dehydrated.'

'Your mum's quite right,' said Mrs. Challendar. 'If you're dehydrated it means you haven't got enough fluid in your body. It can make you very ill. It's sensible to drink a lot of water in hot weather.'

Laura got through the day. She was very grumpy but she made it to home time. Later that evening the family was watching television when the weather forecast came on.

'Make the most of this hot spell,' said the weather lady, beaming from the screen, 'because it's not going to last much longer. There's an area of low pressure moving in from the Atlantic and it will bring wet weather and lower temperatures to us all by Friday.

Laura couldn't believe it.

'It's not fair,' she moaned. 'Just as we break up from school. It's been brilliant this weather and now it's going to rain! It's just not fair!'

'I thought you were too hot and sticky?' said mum. 'You haven't stopped complaining.'

'Rubbish!' said Laura. 'I love the hot weather!' and she sat back in her chair and pulled a face at the weather lady.

Prayer: We thank you, Lord, for the wonderful world that you have made. We thank you for summer days when the sun is shining and the sky is blue. We thank you for all the summer school activities such as sports days and school trips. Help us to appreciate how lucky we are and to make the most of our lives by following your example. Amen.

Follow up: The children could write summer poems that could be used for display or read out in a subsequent assembly. A good starting point is to use the five senses. What can they see on a hot summer's day, what can they hear, what can they smell, what do they like to eat or drink, what does the sun feel like as it touches their skin? Each line of the poem could begin with the words:

'On a hot summer's day . . .'

The children could design and draw posters telling others to take care in the sun. The posters could be shown in assembly or displayed around school.

SCHOOL SPORTS DAY

Theme: Competition

Introduction: An obvious time to use this assembly is during the week leading up to School Sports Day. The idea is to keep Sports Day in perspective - particularly for those children who do not display an aptitude for sport - and to promote a spirit of competitive fairness. Explain to the children that, as they live their lives, they will constantly face competition. They cannot always win, nor is it good for them to always come out on top. Someone who, for example, is the fastest runner in one school could come last in a race against runners from other schools. Success has to be kept in perspective. What is important is to do your best, never to boast about achievements and to encourage those who are less talented in a particular area. This advice is particularly relevant as School Sports Day approaches.

The build up to the Broadoak Primary School Sports Day had begun. Mrs. Braddock, the teacher in charge of P.E., had done her best to accommodate all of the children. It had been quite a job for there were two classes in each year group at Broadoak. Children who did not show a particular aptitude for competitive sports were allowed to do demonstration games whilst the rest of the children were allocated events.

There had always been great rivalry between the classes on Sports Day, especially the older juniors in the Year 6 classes. This particular year was no exception. In fact, the rivalry was greater than ever. The two classes were named after the teachers who took them. Mrs. Marsden took one class and so it was known as Year 6M. The other class was Year 6W as their teacher was called Mr. Willis. Peter Jackson was the fastest runner in Year 6M while his great rival from Year 6W was Michael Lever. The boys were not really enemies. In fact, they had both played together for the school football team and they had always got on quite well, without being close friends. However, as Sports Day grew closer, so the rivalry grew more intense.

On the Monday morning of Sports Day week the events were announced. As expected, both Peter and Michael had been entered for the same event, the last race of the afternoon, the distance race that took them two full circuits of the running track.

'You haven't got a chance,' said Peter, as they waited in the dinner queue that lunchtime. 'You may as well pull out now.'

'We'll see about that,' said Michael. 'I'll give you a wave on Thursday as I cross the line in front of you.'

The pressure built up all week. Naturally, the children from 6M wanted Peter to win whilst Michael had the full support of all in 6W. The two boys trained each lunch time, circuit after circuit of the school field, the other children cheering them on and chanting their names. The lunchtime supervisors thought it was wonderful. Everyone was so busy concentrating on Sports Day that there were no arguments for days!

Thursday arrived. The weather was just right. It was dry but it was not too hot. There was a thin covering of light grey cloud. Conditions were perfect. The excitement grew throughout the morning. Year 6 children helped Mrs. Braddock carry equipment out and set up the school field. Chairs were taken out for parents and visitors. Peter and Michael were both looking confident.

'I'm feeling really fit,' announced Peter, as he carried out a box of bean bags. He made sure that Michael was within hearing distance. 'This race should be a piece of cake!'

'I'm faster than ever this year,' returned Michael. 'I can't wait to get my winner's certificate from Mrs. Braddock!'

The afternoon got off to a good start. There was a large crowd of enthusiastic spectators. The atmosphere was excellent. Laura Cross got stuck going under the net in the obstacle race and Mrs. Braddock and two other teachers had to untangle her. Laura saw the funny side; she couldn't stop laughing! One of the Year 3 boys put his foot in the bucket during the bucket and bean bag race. He couldn't get it out so he finished the race with a bucket on his foot! Generally, however, the events went smoothly.

At twenty minutes past three, after a really good afternoon, it was time for the big race. The distance race was for both boys and girls, twelve children in total. Peter found a starting position towards the middle of the track and Michael immediately lined up alongside him. The spectators started clapping rhythmically and then they fell silent as the starter got the runners prepared. After a tense few seconds there was a single blast on a whistle and the runners set off. There were a few bumps and bangs as the children jostled for position but the race soon settled down. Peter dropped into fourth position, running easily, maintaining a steady pace. Michael was in fifth, right

behind him, ready to strike. The spectators were going wild.

'Pee-ter! Pee-ter!' chanted 6M.
'Mich-ael! Mich-ael!' retorted 6W.

At the end of the first lap, Peter was in second place and Michael was right on his heels in third. The chants got louder. The spectators waved their arms in the air, urging on their favourite.

Then Peter hit the front. He made his move and for a moment he pulled away from Michael. The children from 6M went wild. One girl fell off her chair in excitement. But Michael responded. With a sudden burst of speed he was at Peter's shoulder. There was less than half a lap to go. And then he was level. The two rivals were side by side and there was nothing between them. Lucy Howarth was in third place but she was five metres behind the two boys. The finishing line was in sight and there was still nothing between them. They were shoulder to shoulder. They gave every last ounce of effort, pushing themselves on towards the line. The finishing tape was in sight when . . . it happened. The two boys were so close to each other that their feet tangled. In one split second they lurched forward and crashed to the ground, just metres from the finishing line. The spectators let out a gasp of amazement, but Lucy Howarth took her chance. She charged past the two boys, her arms raised in a victory salute. Nine other children cantered home. Peter and Michael picked themselves up and staggered over the line together. They were the last two to finish.

It took them a few minutes to recover. They sat next to each other on the grass and, eventually, when he had got his breath back, Michael said, 'Never mind, Peter, it was a good race!'

'Yes, it was a good race,' agreed Peter. 'That's all that really matters. It was a good race!'

And the two boys shook hands and grinned at each other before pulling themselves to their feet and walking across to congratulate Lucy Howarth on her victory in the big race.

Prayer: Help us, Lord, to do our best in everything we do. Teach us that winning is not everything in this competitive life. Kindness and consideration for others is just as important. May we learn to compete fairly and accept our position in life graciously. Amen.

Follow up: The story provides several points for discussion. How did Peter and Michael feel towards each other prior to the big race? How did they behave? How did the other children contribute towards the rivalry? How did they behave after the race?

It is important to stress that competition is fine if it is conducted with good spirit and in a fair and appropriate manner. You may wish to discuss the behaviour of modern sports men and women. Do they set a good example? Are they appropriate role models?

Discuss other areas in life where the children will face competition. (e.g. examinations, competition for school places, job interviews etc.).

BROUGH STREET'S BAD WEEK

Theme: Behaving in an acceptable manner

Introduction: Ask the children why they think it is necessary to have school rules? What would school be like if there were no rules? Apart from the fact that there would be general chaos, with everyone doing exactly as they pleased, school would be a dangerous place. Rules are in place to help everyone and it is everyone's responsibility to make sure that the rules are followed. This is especially important in the school environment in order to ensure that everyone is cared for properly and that all children make the best possible progress in both work and behaviour.

It had been a bad day at Brough Street Primary School. Yes, it was a Friday towards the end of a long, hard term and everyone was tired. Furthermore, it had been raining virtually non-stop all week, so that the children had not been able to play out - but that was no excuse for such a bad week and both staff and children knew it.

The week had got off to a bad start on the Monday morning. The playground was soaking wet and there were puddles of water everywhere. Some of the boys decided that it would be a good idea to jump in the puddles and see how far they could kick the water. Unfortunately, apart from making themselves soaking wet, they kicked the water over some of the Nursery parents who were delivering their children to class. The parents were fuming and they stormed into school to see Mrs. Watson, the Headteacher. Mrs. Watson was not pleased to have to deal with a complaint first thing on Monday morning. She sent for the offending boys and made them apologise to the angry parents.

The rain came down heavier during the morning and the children could not go out for play. Most classes had 'wet playtime games' and the system usually worked very well. However, Mrs. Banks, the Year 2 teacher, was called away for a phone call during playtime and, although she had left monitors in charge, when she got back to class the room was in a terrible mess. The games had been scattered everywhere and it took ten minutes to clear away.

Another of the classes got into trouble on Wednesday lunchtime. Some children from Year 4 were very cheeky to the lunchtime supervisors. They were sent straight to Mrs. Watson. If there was one thing Mrs. Watson could not stand it was children who were rude and cheeky. Again, the offending children had to apologise and they were told that they had to stand outside Mrs. Watson's room each playtime and dinner time for the rest of the week.

The children got out briefly on Thursday lunchtime - just long enough for a group of Year 5 children to get involved in a fight. As usual, it was about something and nothing. A couple of children were chasing after each other and they accidentally bumped into some others playing a different game. Tempers flared quickly and the lunchtime supervisors had to intervene before the situation got out of hand.

'I don't know,' sighed Mrs. Watson, as the guilty children stood before her, heads bowed, 'the first time you are able to play out this week and you're sent in for squabbling! Not a very good example to set for the younger children, is it?'

Clearly, it had been a bad week at Brough Street Primary School. Mrs. Watson stood sternly at the front of the hall for Friday afternoon assembly. The children seemed to sense that she was not pleased and the teachers sat quietly, arms folded. They knew what was coming.

The Headteacher began. 'I am very disappointed with you all this week.' She removed her glasses and stared slowly around the hall, waiting for the words to take effect. 'I think you all know that general behaviour in and around school has not been acceptable, don't you?'

The question was rhetorical. She did not expect a reply but Joshua Harris from Reception class said, 'Yes, Mrs. Watson!'

'Thank you, Joshua. I'm glad you agree. Now I am sure that many of you have not enjoyed this school week as much as you should have done. When school is orderly and children are well behaved there is a much more pleasant atmosphere, isn't there?'

'Yes, Mrs. Watson!' Joshua was nodding his head up and down.

'When you behave badly the teachers end up cross and everyone feels grumpy. Is it fair that the teachers should feel grumpy when they are trying to look after you and help you learn?'

Mrs. Watson stared down at Joshua just as he was about to answer.

'I don't think it is fair, is it? I think each and every one of you should make a promise - a determined effort to come to school with a smile on your faces on Monday morning and to behave well all week. Let us make sure that next week at Brough Street Primary School is a really good week. Shall we do that?'

'Yes, Mrs. Watson!' agreed Joshua, and he looked round at the other children with a huge smile on his face.

Prayer: A happy and a hard working school is everyone's responsibility. Help us, Lord, to behave in an acceptable manner at all times. Teach us the difference between right and wrong. May we grow up to be kind and considerate people who show self control and who are sensitive to the needs of other people. May we live our lives as you would have us. Amen.

Follow up: Discuss the concept that everyone is responsible for a happy and successful school. Is it necessary to have rules if this aim is to be achieved? Discuss some of the existing school rules. Are the rules effective? Can children suggest any additional rules that would improve life in school? Do children think any of the rules are unnecessary? What should happen to people who break the rules?

It is just as important to have rules in society. Who is responsible for making rules in society? Who ensures that the rules are kept? What would happen if there were no rules and everyone could do as they pleased?

UNRELIABLE RICK

Theme: Keeping your word/Reliability

Introduction: Ask the children what the word reliable means. Explain that when teachers look for children to do jobs in class or around school, they choose children who are reliable; children they can depend on to do a job properly; children they know will not let them down. It is the same when you grow older and start applying for jobs. Employers ask for references from schools and colleges so that they know what you are like. An employer is unlikely to offer a job to someone who cannot arrive on time or who puts off a task because he or she can't be bothered to complete it properly. You are never too young to start being reliable. If you say you are going to do something - then do it!

Rick finally handed in his maths homework two days late. Mrs. Taylor, his class teacher, was not pleased.

'I asked for this work to be in on Monday morning, Rick - not Wednesday afternoon. Would you like to explain why it is so late?'

'I forgot to put it in my school bag,' lied Rick. He had completed it that lunchtime in the school playground. 'I only remembered this morning.'

The rest of the class sat in silence as the drama unfolded.

'Well, it's not good enough, is it, Rick? What if I forgot to mark all your books, or I forgot to bring them back to school on time? What if I forgot to let you out at playtime? You wouldn't like it, would you Rick?'

'No, Mrs. Taylor,' Rick's head was bowed. He was not really ashamed because he was used to being told off.

'Reliability, Rick. Look the word up in the dictionary. Reliability is something you need to acquire and acquire very quickly. Now go and sit down so that we can begin our afternoon lesson.'

Rick was not sure what the word meant and he grabbed a dictionary from the shelf as he made his way back to his table. It was not that Rick wasn't interested in his schoolwork - he just couldn't seem to get himself organised. Rick had taken his maths book home the previous Thursday, when the homework had been set. He had gone up to his bedroom fully intending to do his homework that same evening. The problem was that his bedroom looked like a rubbish tip. It was so untidy that there was nowhere for him to sit and work. His mum had been nagging him for weeks to do something about his room, which she referred to as The Pit.

So Rick began to tidy his room. He moved the half-eaten piece of toast from under his pillow and picked three socks from beneath his quilt. Three socks? Why were there only three? He stuck his head under the quilt to search for the fourth sock. Ah! There was his missing football boot! Mr. Shaw, the Games teacher, had been really annoyed when Rick had turned up to the football practice wearing one boot and one training shoe. Rick dropped the socks and the boot on the floor and continued to burrow beneath his quilt. He found several other interesting items including last week's dinner money and his sister's birthday present. No wonder he'd been uncomfortable in bed. His sister would really like that hairbrush.

Rick was beginning to feel bored. He hated tidying up. He switched on his television and lay down for a rest. He was just in time! The theme music for Blue Peter started and Rick settled back to watch the programme. When it was over, Rick remembered about his maths homework - but he couldn't remember where he had put his book.

'Never mind,' he thought, 'I'll look for it later.'

It was the following Wednesday morning when mum eventually fished Rick's book out of the washing basket. He'd dropped it in there with the three socks.

'What on earth is your maths homework book doing in the washing basket?' stormed mum.

'Look at the state of it! You can't take it into school like that! It smells of old socks!'

'It'll be fine,' said Rick, holding it at arm's length. 'Anyway, Mrs. Taylor's got a cold - she won't notice.'

And so Rick had got into trouble for once again handing in his homework late. He opened the dictionary and searched through for the word reliability. *Reload, reluctant . . . rely!* There it was - 'to depend on with confidence'. Rick knew that Mrs. Taylor could not depend on him - which was why she never chose him to do any of the jobs round the classroom. Maybe it was time he changed. Maybe it was time to make a real effort. Yes - Rick decided it was time he made a real effort. He would begin that very evening by tidying his bedroom properly. From now on he was going to make sure people thought of him as Reliable Rick.

Prayer: As we grow up, Lord, help us to be honest, trustworthy and reliable. May we be the kind of people that others can depend on with confidence and feel they may turn to when they need help or encouragement. May we live our lives by following your example. Amen.

Follow up: For most jobs, reliability is an essential quality. Children rely on teachers to impart knowledge; patients rely on doctors and nurses for effective treatment. Reliability may be linked to good, personal organisation. Discuss how this is encouraged in the daily routine of school life. How is it encouraged at home?

Ask the children whom they rely on most of all and in what way. Discuss all the things for which they rely on their parents e.g. food, clothes, presents, trips out, being woken up for school in the morning! Make a list to show just how much children rely on those who care for them.

I'M NOT FEELING WELL

Theme: Sickness

Introduction: Begin by asking the children: 'Who has been off school ill recently?' If hands are raised, select a few children and ask what was wrong with them. You may wish to recount a time when you were ill and explain to the children how you felt. Nobody likes being ill but there are inevitably times when you will not feel well. It happens to children and it happens to adults and there is very little you can do about it. Usually, with care and attention and perhaps the right medicine, you recover very quickly and you are soon back to normal. Just occasionally, things are more serious and more specialised care is required. Thankfully, there is not too much wrong with the little girl in the story to follow.

Lucy was not feeling well. She had sat in class for most of the morning without saying anything but, just before lunch, she started to feel most peculiar. She was very hot and every time she moved she felt dizzy. She decided she had better tell the teacher but when she tried to stand up her legs went all wobbly and she had to sit down again. Her friend, Sarah, noticed that there was something wrong and she put a steadying hand on Lucy's arm.

'Lucy, what's the matter? You've gone a really funny colour?'

Lucy didn't answer. She put her head down on the desk and took a few deep breaths. Sarah went to the front of class and told Mrs. Abbot, her teacher, immediately. Mrs. Abbot was concerned. Several children had been sent home from school with the same symptoms recently. There was obviously a virus going round.

Five minutes later, Lucy was sitting in the school entrance area waiting for her mum to collect her. Mrs. Myers, the school secretary, had rung Lucy's mum at work and she was on her way.

'I'm sure she'll be all right,' said Mrs. Myers, as Lucy's mum looked at her daughter in concern. 'We've had quite a few children off poorly. It seems to last for about three days.'

'Come on. Let's get you home,' said mum. 'Straight to bed for you, my girl.'

Lucy still felt wobbly as she made her way to the car and she shivered as she went out into the cold air.

'I'm sorry, mum,' she whimpered. 'I really don't feel well.'

'What are you sorry about?' asked mum. 'You can't help being poorly, can you?'

It was not long before Lucy was tucked up in bed. She still felt rotten but she was glad to be home. Lucy's mum made her a cup of tea, which she left by the side of the bed. Lucy took a sip but she really didn't want it. She didn't want anything. She felt really tired and she closed her eyes and drifted off into a deep sleep. Lucy's mum kept popping into the room to check that she was all right and, although Lucy was rather restless, she knew that sleep was the best thing for her.

The following morning, Lucy felt a little better. Her head still ached and she still felt dizzy when she got up to go to the bathroom but she didn't feel as awful as she had done at school. Mum made her a cup of tea and a piece of toast for breakfast. Lucy managed to drink the tea and she ate half of the toast. She stayed in bed and dozed for most of the day but, by evening, she had perked up considerably.

'You're beginning to look human again,' said mum. 'You've got a bit of colour back in your cheeks.'

'Can I come downstairs and watch some television?' asked Lucy. She was sitting up in bed and feeling much livelier.

'I don't see why not,' replied mum. 'Put your dressing gown on and I'll help you down.'

Lucy watched television for a couple of hours and then she felt tired again.

'Come on,' said mum, spotting the signs. 'Another good night's sleep and you'll be as right as rain!'

Mum was right. The following morning, Lucy felt much better. She woke up at her usual time feeling hungry. She got up by herself and went downstairs.

'I'm better!' she proclaimed, with a big smile on her face. 'Can I go back to school today, mum?'

'I think we'll give it one more day,' said mum. 'You haven't eaten properly, yet. And we need to see how you are when you go outside - but I'm sure you'll be back to school tomorrow.'

'I hope so,' said Lucy, sitting down to a bowl of Cornflakes. 'I get bored at home.'

'Funny thing,' said mum, raising her hand to her brow, 'I've got a bit of a headache and I feel a little dizzy!' She sat down on a kitchen chair. 'Do you know, Lucy - you're really kind. You always share whatever you've got!'

Prayer: We thank you, Lord, that we are able to enjoy good health. We thank you for all the things that being fit and healthy enable us to do. We think especially, this morning, of those people who are ill and are not able to live full and active lives. We know that you are with them to offer care and comfort. Amen.

Follow up: It is true that nobody can help being ill - but there is no doubt that a particular lifestyle promotes a healthy mind and a healthy body. What sort of things promote a healthy mind? What sort of lifestyle promotes a healthy body? You could make two lists and see if there is any overlap. (Sleep, for example, is essential for both mind and body).
The children could write from their own experience. Ask them to produce personal accounts of a time they were taken ill. Afterwards, share experiences in a reading session. Some children will have been in hospital, which should interest those who have not had that experience.

Discuss the improvements advances in medicine, health care and hygiene have made to modern life. Compare being ill today to being ill in Victorian times.

DON'T SAY A WORD

Theme: Honesty

Introduction: I am sure that all of you have seen someone in school doing something that you know to be wrong. Sometimes, it may not be too serious. For example, you may see someone going out of bounds to retrieve a football; you may see someone talking in class when the teacher has asked for silence; you may see someone being silly in the dining hall at lunchtime. All of these things are wrong and they are not to be encouraged - but I wonder what you would do if you saw someone doing something really bad. Would you turn a blind eye or would you take some action. Listen to the following story and decide how you would have reacted.

It was Saturday afternoon and Lisa was bored. She had finished her school homework and there was nothing on television that she wanted to watch. Her brother was out playing football and her mum and dad were tidying up the house.

'I've nothing to do,' complained Lisa. 'I'm really bored.'

'Why don't you tidy up your bedroom?' suggested mum. 'That will take you the rest of the weekend!'

'I'm not that desperate,' said Lisa, quickly. 'I think I'll go down to the shop and buy a magazine. I just fancy a good read. I'll be back in a few minutes.'

'OK, off you go then,' said mum. 'Take care.'

The newsagent's was not far away. Lisa strolled along the road, wondering which magazine she would buy. As she reached the shop, her best friend Mel was outside with two older girls Lisa did not recognise.

'Hi, Lisa,' said Mel, cheerfully. 'This is Karen and Abbie. We're going in to town this afternoon. Do you want to come with us?'

'Better not,' replied Lisa. 'My mum will wonder where I am. I told her I wouldn't be long.'

'Suit yourself,' said Karen, giving Lisa an icy stare. 'It's your loss.'

'See you soon,' said Lisa, and she opened the shop door and went inside.

The newsagent's was empty apart from one elderly lady who was chatting away to Mrs. Riley, the shopkeeper. She was leaning over the sweet counter telling Mrs. Riley all about her electricity bill. A large display stand ran down the centre of the shop and the magazines were to the right of it. Lisa smiled at Mrs. Riley and disappeared behind the stand to choose her magazine.

A few moments later the shop door opened and Karen and Abbie entered, Mel following behind. Mel walked straight up to the counter and started to choose some sweets from the various trays. Karen and Abbie slipped around the display stand, nudging each other and giggling. Karen saw Lisa and she raised a finger to her lips, signalling for Lisa to remain quiet - not to say a word. As Lisa looked on in horror, Karen took two pens from a display container and slipped them inside her jacket. She glanced towards the counter. Good! Mel was asking Mrs. Riley how much her sweets would cost. Karen got back to work. She removed a bottle of nail varnish from a tray and put it inside her jacket with the pens.

Lisa stood there with her mouth open. She couldn't believe her eyes. She didn't know what to do.

Abbie reached past her and removed a magazine from the shelf. There was a free C.D. stuck to the front cover. It was the very magazine Lisa was going to buy. Abbie took one look at it and stuffed it inside her jacket.

Lisa heard Mel say, 'Thanks, Mrs. Riley' and she saw the two older girls signal to each other to leave the shop. They moved away from the display stands, smug and satisfied with their work.

At that moment the door opened and a tall, thin gentleman entered the shop.

Karen and Abbie glanced at each other and moved towards the door. Mel joined them and the tall gentleman held the door open for the girls to pass through.

Lisa didn't know what made her do it - but she shook herself and rushed forward. She pushed the door closed and leaned against it as the astonished gentleman looked on. Karen and Abbie exchanged nervous glances. Mel looked horrified. She looked as if she was about to burst into tears. And then Lisa found her voice.

'Stop them, Mr. Riley! You've got to stop them! They've been stealing!'

Prayer: Help us, Lord, to be honest at all times. We know that there will be occasions in our lives when we are tempted to do things we should not do. Help us to be strong. Teach us the difference between right and wrong and give us the courage, the confidence and the determination to make correct decisions. Amen.

Follow up: The story raises several issues for discussion. Ask the children what they think about the way in which Lisa handled the situation? Why was the situation particularly difficult for Lisa? What would they have done in the same situation? What do they think would happen next in the story? What was Mel's role in the plot? Was she as guilty as Karen and Abbie?

Broaden the discussion to other examples of wrongdoing. Is it right to 'turn a blind eye'? There are times when serious crimes are committed, yet witnesses do not come forward. Why do you think this happens? Are people afraid of the consequences or is it that they just do not care?

The children could write their own stories with a similar theme. Perhaps their stories could be given a school setting.

DO YOU REALLY LIKE YOURSELF

Theme: Taking pride in the way you live your life

Introduction: Have the question: Do you really like yourself? written on a whiteboard or flipchart at the front of assembly. Also, have the question: Would you like to be your friend? clearly visible. Begin by asking the children what qualities they look for when choosing a friend. Write down words given, such as honesty, trust, humour etc. All are qualities to be admired. Having talked about the qualities, explain to the children that if they seek such qualities in others then they should strive to achieve the same qualities in their own lives.

There they were, displayed at the front of the school hall for all to see. Two questions printed in large, black letters on a white background:

DO YOU REALLY LIKE YOURSELF? WOULD YOU LIKE TO BE YOUR FRIEND?

'Of course I like myself,' said Pete, as he stared at the sign. 'I think I'm pretty lovely, to be honest.'

'I'd like to be my friend,' confirmed Louise. 'I like the way I look and I like the things I do.'

'They're stupid questions,' continued Pete. 'Nobody's going to admit that they don't like themselves. Nobody with any sense, that is.'

'Yes, stupid questions,' agreed Louise, 'I don't know what they're doing on display in the school hall.'

The two children stared at them for another minute and then turned and made their way back to class.

Later that morning there was a maths test. Louise knew that maths was not her best subject but, to make matters worse, she had not done any revision for the test. She had taken her books home but other things had seemed more important - such as watching television and playing on her computer. When Louise saw the questions, she was horrified. She knew that she should have been able to cope with the test and she knew that, if she had just spent a little time revising, she would have been able to have a go at it. However, she stared at the test paper and did not know where to begin. To make matters worse, she was sitting next to Ayesha, who was the best in the class at maths. Ayesha was already busy writing and Louise could see that she was on the third question. And then, to her surprise, Louise realised that she could also see Ayesha's answers. She glanced to the front of the class. Mrs. Hill was busy marking some books. Louise picked up her pen and set to work, glancing sideways every so often to confirm the answers. It was easy! She was going to do well in her maths test after all!

It was dinner time and Pete was surprised to find that he was the first pupil in the dining hall. He walked across to the serving trolley to see what was on offer for lunch. The dinner ladies were still in the kitchen, rushing around with pots and pans and tea towels. Suddenly, something caught Pete's eye. There, beneath the trolley, was a one pound coin. Pete looked around. There was no sign of anybody. He stooped down and picked up the coin. He held it in his hand for a moment and then he slipped it in his pocket.

'What a bit of luck!' he thought. 'No one will ever know!'

The hall doors burst open and a stream of children entered the room, chattering and laughing, ready to devour their mid day meals. Pete smiled in satisfaction and waited at the front of the queue.

After lunch, Pete was playing football with a group of his friends in the school yard. There was no doubt that Pete was a good footballer. He played in the centre of defence for the school team. He could tackle hard and he could pass the ball well. Daniel Harris was new to the school. He had joined Pete's class earlier that same week and he was still settling in. Seeing the game of football in progress, and realising that it was Pete's ball they were playing with, Daniel shouted across to Pete: 'Do you mind if I join in?'

'Yes, I do mind!' snapped Pete. 'We've got enough playing. Go and find your own friends!'

Daniel turned away and wandered across the yard. He was clearly hurt.

That afternoon Mrs. Hill gave out the results of the maths test. Ayesha had scored the highest marks but Louise was only just behind her.

'Excellent work, Louise,' said Mrs. Hill, as she handed back the test papers. 'You have clearly worked very hard for this test. I think you deserve a reward for making such good progress.'

Louise took her paper and smiled weakly. She had a strange feeling deep inside and she was not sure that she liked it.

Pete and Louise stared at the two bold questions displayed at the front of the school hall. It was the end of the school day and they had their coats on as they were on their way home.

Pete put his hand in his pocket and felt the one pound coin. Daniel, the new boy, walked across the school hall behind him.

'I think I know what those questions mean,' said Pete, quietly.

'I have to admit, they do make you think,' said Louise. She was clutching her school bag, which contained her maths books. Louise had decided to take them home and revise.

'When I think about it, there are one or two things that make me wonder if I really would like to be my friend,' said Pete, and then he turned round and hurried after Daniel to see if he wanted some company on his way home.

Prayer: Help us to live our lives in an honest and trustworthy manner. May we never say or do anything of which we are ashamed. As we grow up, may we be kind and thoughtful people who give full consideration to those around us. Amen.

Follow up: The story raises important issues for discussion. What should Pete have done when he found the one pound coin on the hall floor? Why was he wrong not to allow Daniel to join in his game of football? What should you do when a new pupil joins the school? Louise had a strange feeling when Mrs. Hill handed back her maths test and praised her for doing so well. What was this feeling? If you have a 'guilty conscience', what does it tell you?

A good rule to live by is: Always treat others as you yourself would wish to be treated. Discuss this concept. Have you ever said or done anything that you really regretted? Is it true that you sometimes hurt the people you care about most?